Beyond the Storm

A JOURNEY OF TURNING PAIN INTO POWER

By Latricia Ferris

Beyond the Storm

A Journey of Turning Pain into Power

By Latricia Ferris

Beyond the Storm
A Journey of Turning Pain into Power © 2025 by Latricia
Ferris

All rights reserved.

This is a work of nonfiction. The stories and events
shared are based on the lived experiences of the author.
While some names and identifying details have been
changed to protect privacy, the essence of each account
remains true to its emotional and historical reality.

For permissions, speaking engagements, or
inquiries, please contact:

Latricia Ferris
Dream, Believe & Imagine Incorporated Denver,
Colorado www.dreambelieveimagine.com

Cover design, interior layout, and all original content
by Latricia Ferris.

ISBN (Hardcover): 979-8-9931867-0-2 ISBN
(Paperback): 979-8-9931867-1-9 ISBN (eBook): 979-8-
9931867-2-6 Library of Congress Control Number:

2025922138

Latricia Ferris

First Edition, 2025
Printed in the United States of America

Published by Dream, Believe & Imagine Publishing

Dedication

To Danajha, Aron Jr, and J'Honesty, my babies, my light, my reason. You didn't just change my life. You shaped it for the better. Every page of this book carries the strength you helped me find.

To my bonus babies, Amauri, Anthony, and Jakhi. Loving you came naturally. Thank you for letting me show up in your lives with open arms and an open heart. You've expanded my purpose in ways I never knew I needed.

To Aron Sr., despite everything, our friendship and love have stood the test of time. Thank you for being part of the foundation.

To my parents, Chester and Charlene. You gave me life, and through every storm, you gave me lessons that made this woman possible.

To my Granny Patricia. Your love and wisdom live in me. Still. Always.

To my siblings, Tia, Josh, Isaac, and Isaiah. We were forged in the same fire. You are my first tribe. My forever.

To Dana and Fatso. You were part of the village that raised me when I didn't even know I needed one.

To Joanna Hughes. My first business mentor. You saw something in me before I fully saw it in myself. Thank you for opening doors and reminding me to walk through them boldly.

And to the attendees of my pre-launch event. You were there when this dream was still trembling in my chest. You believed. You witnessed. You helped shape this story. Your names and your impact will never be forgotten.

Jeanetta "Stormy" James, Tia Combs, Summer Nettles, Shirley Sullen,

Danajha Walker, Amauri Walker, Aron Walker, Sariah King, Mya Warren,

Garey Thompson, Katrena Chase, Lauren Lockard, Marcus Ferrell,

Carol Robinson, Thomas Greer, Sara Wisdom, Jeanette Wu,

Janelle Hartvigsen, Lewis Brown, Aurora Elicerio, and Brandee Brown.

vii

Introduction

"The storm may shake you, but it can never erase the light you were born with."

This book is not meant to be rushed through. It is meant to be felt.

Beyond the Storm is more than a memoir. It is a living, breathing testimony of what it means to fall apart, rebuild, and rise again. Every page carries fragments of my soul, pieces of the girl I once was, and echoes of the woman I have become.

Each chapter is named after a storm because that is what life has been: seasons of thunder and calm, destruction and renewal, heartbreak and rebirth. Some storms came roaring, shaking everything I thought was stable. Others crept in like fog, soft and silent, but still powerful enough to change the shape of my life.

But here is what I learned. Storms do not just come to destroy. They come to clear the path, to reveal the strength you did not know you had, and to water the seeds buried deep within you.

Every story in these pages is a reflection of that truth. Within each storm, you will find moments of breaking and rebuilding. There are stories of love and loss, of motherhood and miracles, of betrayal and forgiveness. There are days when the rain feels endless and nights when I almost forget how to pray. But there are also mornings filled with sunlight and laughter that returned after I thought joy was gone forever.

Inside each chapter, you will find:

- A storm-themed **quote** and **affirmation** to ground your spirit.

- A **raw, unfiltered story** from my life, told with truth and heart.

- A **reflection page** with tools and journal prompts to help you process your own emotions and heal as you read.

- A closing **"After the Storm"** section that shows how pain transformed into power, how healing became purpose, and how purpose gave birth to peace.

This book is not only about what I have been through. It is about what I became because of it.

It is about resilience, the kind that does not just survive the fire but learns to dance in its glow.

If you have ever endured betrayal, heartbreak, loss, or silence that felt like it might swallow you whole, this book is for you. If you have ever questioned why God allowed the storm, I want you to know this. He was not punishing you. He was preparing you.

Every scar you carry tells a story, and every story holds power. The pain was never meant to define you. It was meant to refine you.

When you read these chapters, take your time. Sit with the words. Let them breathe life into your weary places. Allow yourself to cry, to laugh, to feel everything you have been holding in. Healing is not a straight line. It is a series of waves, and this book will meet you wherever you are in the tide.

Beyond the Storm is an invitation to remember your worth, to reclaim your peace, and to rediscover your power.

You will see yourself in these pages. The broken parts, the brave parts, the divine parts that refused to give up. And by the end, I hope you see what I finally learned.
That no matter how fierce the winds, no matter how heavy the rain, the sun will rise again.

You are not alone.
You are not forgotten.
You are not too damaged to bloom.

You are the storm and the calm after it.
You are the phoenix and the flame.
You are proof that beauty lives even in the aftermath.

So, take a deep breath, turn the page, and let the healing begin. You are stronger than any storm, and you always were.

" Latricia Ferris

Healing isn't pretty, but it's real, and real always outlast perfect

Beyond the Storm "

When the Storms Come

They say some people are born in the calm. I was not one of them.

I was born with thunder in my ears and broken glass under my feet. I grew up learning to listen for footsteps, to read the air before a door slammed, to shield my siblings from chaos I could not control.

Before I ever learned long division, I learned how to divide trauma into manageable pieces. Before I could spell "resilience," I was already embodying it.

This book is not fiction. It is not dramatized. And it is not for the faint of heart.

This is real life.

These are the stories I was never supposed to tell. Stories of abandonment, addiction, sexual assault, kidnapping, cancer, grief, betrayal, and survival. Stories I carried silently because nobody ever asked. Because I thought nobody would understand. Because silence felt safer than rejection.

But I have learned that silence does not save us. It stains us. Unspoken pain becomes generational until somebody breaks the chain.

I chose to be that somebody.

This book is for those who have survived without applause. For those who became parents too soon. For those who still carry invisible bruises. For the leaders who had to lead from broken places.

Each chapter is named after a storm. Every season of my life, no matter how dark, left behind something sacred: wisdom, skill, grit, compassion, fire.

Every storm tried to take something from me. But I took something back.

I turned pain into power. I turned trauma into truth. And now I am telling it all. Not to relive the wounds, but to reclaim them.

I refuse to let the worst things that ever happened to me have the final say.

This is not a book of victimhood. This is a book of becoming.

If you are reading this, maybe it is time for you to become one too.

So let the first storm roll

Some storms come to destroy what's false, so truth can finally breathe

Thunderstorm Cell Formation

"Not all storms come to disrupt your life; some come to clear your path."

Affirmation: The storm that was meant to break me built a fire inside me that no one can put out.

The building block of every thunderstorm is the thunderstorm cell. Most last only about thirty minutes. Some storms come quietly, sliding in on heavy air and thick skies. Others rage with warning, cracking the heavens open. Either way, when the clouds form, everything you thought was certain starts to tremble.

That's how my storm came. Soft at first. It was slow, creeping, scattered across neighborhoods and years. Even before I knew what trauma was, it was already building inside of me.

I spent my earliest years in the projects on the east side of Denver, better known as the Red Bricks. Our unit sat in a row of brick buildings with narrow walkways, the kind of place where the walls were thin and the drama was thick.

From the outside, they looked like tired row houses, with red brick walls stacked in lines, concrete stairs that were always cold beneath bare feet, and kitchens and living rooms

2

squeezed together downstairs, while bathrooms and bedrooms were tucked upstairs. It was crowded, noisy, alive.

Every corner of those buildings carried a story; some whispered, some shouted, some hid behind doors that we knew better than to open.

Mornings began with music. My parents played vinyl on a record player that always seemed a little scratched, and Michael Jackson was the soundtrack to our lives. His voice poured out of the speakers while sunlight slipped through thin curtains.

"Don't Stop 'Til You Get Enough" spun while we ate cereal or hot breakfast, and sometimes, if Mama was in a good mood, we'd get soul food, grits, bacon, biscuits that filled the air with warmth and love. The smell of fried chicken or collard greens on Sundays seeped into the walls, reminding us that no matter how tough life was outside, inside, we still knew comfort. Sometimes those mornings felt like a celebration, even if all we had was the crackle of vinyl and the sizzle of food in a skillet. They were little moments of sunshine breaking through thick clouds.

Our neighbors became part of the fabric of my memory. An older woman lived next door. She was visually impaired, but to me, she was simply kind. Her voice was steady, her laugh gentle, and she always asked how we were doing.

Across the walkway lived a family with five kids. One of their older daughters, ReOnna, came over so often that she called my parents "Mom" and "Dad."

3

It wasn't strange, it was love. She's still my sister in every way that matters. The Red Bricks had a way of weaving people into your family, whether by blood or bond. There were no clear lines between whose kid belonged to whom. We belonged to each other, even when times were hard.

The soundtrack of the projects wasn't just Michael Jackson. It was the Electric Slide blasting from speakers at weekend gatherings, the shuffle of feet on concrete, laughter spilling across the courtyards. Kids played double-dutch and tag, their shouts mixing with the sharp cracks of arguments after too much beer was poured. The nights carried every sound: children playing, lovers fighting, mothers calling their kids in from the dark, sirens wailing in the distance like an unwanted lullaby. Even in the chaos, there was rhythm, a strange harmony in the noise, as if the neighborhood were a living, breathing organism, pulsing with both joy and pain.

We had our adventures. A penny candy store sat just a few blocks away, the kind of place where a single dollar made you rich. We would count out our coins carefully, palms sweating with excitement, then walk the cracked sidewalks to buy Now and Laters, Lemonheads, and the kind of candy that left your tongue red for hours. The walk itself was an adventure, full of dodging cracks in the pavement, calling out to friends, and holding each other's hands when the street felt too wide. The metal playground on the property was our kingdom. Hot in the summer, cold in the winter, it didn't matter; we climbed, swung, and jumped until our knees were skinned and our hands blistered.

On good days, Grandma would take us on the RTD bus to the Goodwill. The ride felt like forever, with the bus rumbling under us and the city flashing by the windows, but with her at the front of the bus, sharp and determined, it always felt safe. We'd search for clothes or treasures, her voice bartering with clerks, her laughter filling the aisles as she found us something new to wear. That bus ride wasn't just about thrift shopping; it was about being reminded that even when we had little, we still had enough.

One afternoon in the west Denver townhouse when I was six, I was left to watch my siblings, and I decided to play "Follow the Leader." There was a big, broken glass Deep Rock jug tucked in the corner of the basement. I don't know what made me do it, but I stuck my foot in. It came back out fine. Tia followed me and did the same. But when Josh put his four-year-old foot in, the glass snapped and cut deep into his ankle.

Blood everywhere. Screams echoed through the basement.

"Tricia! He's bleeding!" Tia shrieked; her voice sharp with panic. She grabbed a rag and tried to hide the blood, as if covering it would erase what had happened.

Josh cried, but he was too little to understand the danger. Brave in his own way, his tears mixed with confusion more than fear. He whimpered but didn't scream the way I expected. His wide eyes just looked at me, like he was waiting for me to fix it.

My body froze. My hands shook as I pressed a towel against his ankle, my heart pounding in my throat. The blood kept seeping through, red against white, and I wondered if I had just broken something in him that couldn't be fixed.

I grabbed the phone and called Grandma. My voice cracked as I tried to explain. "Josh cut his leg, it won't stop, there's blood everywhere."

When Grandma arrived, her face was a storm. She didn't drive, so she had brought her sister, my Auntie Redd. Auntie Redd stepped out of the car, cursing before she even reached the door. She was old-school gangsta, never sugar-coating a word. "What the hell y'all doing, playing with glass?" she snapped, but her voice carried more fear than anger.

Grandma tried to stay calm, but I could see the fire in her eyes. "Lord, have mercy, girl. You can't play like that," she said, her hands steady as she wrapped Josh's leg. Her calm steadied me, but the disappointment in her tone cut deep. I had been told from a young age: if my siblings got into trouble, it was on me. I was the oldest. I was in charge. And this time, I had failed.

We rushed Josh to the hospital. The ER was crowded, buzzing with nurses, the smell of antiseptic mixed with sweat and fear.

I sat there, small in a chair that felt too big, praying silently that my little brother wouldn't die because of me. The needle they used for stitches looked huge, like it could pierce through bone. I turned away, unable to watch. But when it was done, Josh looked down at his leg, grinned through drying tears, and said, "I look like Frankenstein!" For a moment, relief washed over me so strongly it almost knocked me down. He even joked he would do it again. Mama didn't laugh. She warned him, "Boy, you try that again and you'll get your butt whooped."

I carried guilt home with me that night, guilt heavy enough to press on my chest like a storm cloud.

It was the first time I truly understood that storms don't always announce themselves with thunder. Sometimes, they creep in quietly, through broken glass and childhood games.

By seven, we moved again. My dad had relocated to California for work, but he bought us a house in a mostly white neighborhood in South Denver.

It looked different from the Red Bricks, cleaner, neater, with manicured lawns and sidewalks that didn't crack beneath your feet. Even though the houses were brighter, the air felt heavier. The neighbors didn't speak. Their eyes followed us, but their words never came. Even as a child, I knew: we were different, and we weren't welcome.

Inside the house, life wasn't calmer. My mom drank more, especially when my dad was away. Strange men came and went. The laughter from behind closed doors was sharp, the bottles on the counter empty. Secrets lived in those walls, and I carried the weight of them even when no one spoke.

I was told over and over: if something happened while my siblings were with me, it was my fault. "If they get in trouble, you're the one who's gonna get it," Mama would say. And I believed her. Responsibility was branded onto me long before I could spell the word.

Still, there were moments of kindness. One neighbor, Aunt Cathy, who was Hispanic, made fresh tortillas for us. She pressed the dough with her hands, laid it on a hot skillet, and handed it to us warm.

We'd eat them with butter, the soft bread melting in our mouths. In those small moments, I felt seen, cared for. But most of the time, the stares from other kids and adults reminded me I didn't belong.

On the bus to school, I sat quietly, clutching my backpack, hearing whispers behind me. In the classroom, kids glanced my way, their eyes lingering too long. I didn't have to hear the words to know what they meant.

The storm of not fitting in sat heavily in my stomach every day.

When the world outside felt unbearable, I built another inside. My sister Tia and I would sit cross-legged on my bedroom floor, the soft scent of baby lotion and crayon wax filling the air.

We played with Barbies for hours, crafting stories where we had power, choice, and freedom.

Tia's Barbie stayed home, nurturing and soft. Mine wore pink high heels and marched into courtrooms as a fierce attorney, winning cases and building a life no storm could touch.

It was exactly like the Barbie movie, bright, glittering, full of possibility. Barbie's world was one where women were strong, where dreams come true, and where chaos didn't exist unless we created it. I loved it because it was the opposite of what I saw around me.

In Barbie's world, no man stumbled in drunk. No mother disappeared behind closed doors. No kids were left to carry responsibilities too heavy for their shoulders.

In that world, I was in control.

But even in those bright moments, the storm lingered. It was in the way my stomach knotted when I heard footsteps that didn't sound familiar. It was in the way I scanned faces, trying to predict danger before it arrived. It was in the way my body never fully relaxed, even when Michael Jackson was spinning on the record player or we were laughing on the playground. I was always waiting, always braced for the moment the sky would split open.

The days felt endless. Warm summer air drifted through open windows, a radio hummed low in the background, and the comforting creak of the house settled around us. I was the firstborn, the trailblazer of our tribe of five.

Tia, my tiny firecracker of a sister, only a year behind me, could throw a punch harder than some grown men. Josh, the mischievous middle child, wore trouble like a second skin. The twins, Isaac and Isaiah, were born minutes apart but bonded like they shared one heart, wild, protective, untamed. Our house was small, our hearts were big, and our dreams were bigger.

But no matter how bright the sun shines, the storm is always waiting just beyond the horizon.

Those early years were not just childhood. They were training. Every laugh, every scraped knee, every long night became another storm cloud forming above me. And even though I didn't know it yet, those storms were not random.

They were cells forming, one after another, each carrying the weight of thunder that would one day strike.

This was the beginning of my thunderstorm cell formation, a storm that was already shaping the girl who would learn to survive it all.

Finding Your Inner Shelter
Pause. Breathe. Reflect.

Storms will come. Not every one gives a warning. Not every one leaves quickly. Some strike like lightning out of a clear sky, shocking us into silence. Others roll in slowly, their clouds thick and heavy until the downpour begins. But no matter how strong the winds howl, you have the power to create shelter inside yourself.

When the world feels unpredictable, your inner shelter becomes your anchor. It does not mean you ignore the storm outside; it means you prepare a place within where peace can survive, even when chaos is everywhere else. Your shelter might be prayer, meditation, journaling, music, or the steady presence of someone who loves you. It is not about walls that shut life out, but foundations that keep you steady when the ground shakes beneath you.

Think of it like a house you carry in your spirit. The roof may be your faith. The walls may be your resilience. The windows may be the hope that lets in light even when the sky outside is dark. And the door? That is your choice: to open it to love, healing, and growth, or to keep it shut against voices that bring destruction. This shelter is yours to build, and it cannot be taken away.

Take a moment to reflect:

Journal Prompt 1: What was one moment in your life when you felt the storm hit? Describe where you were, what you saw, and what you felt in your body. Did your breath shorten? Did your chest tighten? Did you want to run, or freeze? Write it down in vivid detail. Naming it gives you power over it.

Journal Prompt 2: What did that storm take from you? Was it innocence, safety, trust, or hope? Sometimes we hesitate to admit what was stolen because it feels like weakness, but honesty is strength. Say it out loud. Write it down. Release the silence around it.

Journal Prompt 3: What did that storm leave behind that you didn't expect? Storms strip us down, but they also leave deposits behind. Maybe it was resilience you didn't know you had. Maybe it was empathy, compassion, or a deeper understanding of what it means to survive. The storm that broke you also built you. Acknowledge the hidden gifts left behind in the rubble.

Journal Prompt 4: When you look at yourself now, how has that storm shaped you? Be honest. You can mourn and still honor your survival. You can grieve the little girl or boy who lost something precious and still stand proud as the adult who rose anyway. Write about how your choices, your strength, and your wisdom today are shaped by what you once endured. Let yourself see both the wound and the growth.

Take your time with these questions. Do not rush to finish. Sit with them like you would sit with a trusted friend. Breathe between answers. If tears come, let them fall. If anger rises, give it a name. Every emotion is part of your shelter, being built stronger.

Power Statement: *I am my own shelter. No matter what storms rage around me, I carry peace, strength, and safety within. I am not defined by what I lost, but by what I continue to build. Every storm only proves that my foundation cannot be shaken.*

Carry this truth with you as you turn the page. The storm may form again, but so will your strength. And each time you face it, your shelter grows wider, taller, and more unshakable. You are not just surviving; you are becoming the shelter itself.

Latricia Ferris

I walked through thunder and came out shining like lightning

Beyond the Storm

After the Storm: Built in the Eye of the Storm

"What once kept me alive in chaos now guides me in purpose. The storm sharpened my vision long before the world saw my strength."

Affirmation: I trust my instincts. I honor the wisdom I gained in the storm, and I use it to lead with clarity, courage, and truth.

Even in the chaos of my childhood, something was being built inside me. While the world around me spun wild and unpredictable, I was learning how to lead, how to protect, and how to read danger before it struck. That first storm laid the foundation for who I would become.

Learning to Read Energy

I can still remember the way my body would tense when voices shifted in tone. A laugh could turn sharp in an instant, and I had to know when to grab my siblings 'hands and lead them out of the room. The sound of footsteps down the hall, the creak of a door, the sudden pause in a conversation, those were my alarms. My body reacted before my mind had time to catch up.

I learned to watch eyes more than lips, to sense energy more than words. If my mother's gaze drifted just a little too long, if her jaw clenched, I knew the night could spiral quickly. That skill didn't fade as I grew older. Today, when I walk into a boardroom or a leadership meeting, I notice things others overlook. I can tell when someone at the table is pretending to agree but is ready to undercut the plan later. I can feel when a colleague is carrying unspoken frustration that, if ignored, will explode at the wrong moment.

I recall being in a meeting where the PowerPoint presentation glowed brightly, with numbers and charts lined up to make everything appear smooth. But the silence pressed heavily against the walls. Smiles were stretched thin, hands tapped pens too fast, and I knew the real conversation had not yet begun. I leaned in, asked the question no one else would, and the room shifted. Eyes darted, truth cracked open, and the decision was made on honesty instead of politics.

Those instincts once kept my family safe. Now, they allow me to navigate corporate rooms, community boards, and mentorship spaces with precision. What used to be survival has become one of my greatest leadership strengths.

Early Leadership in Chaos

Being the oldest of five meant I never got to be "just a kid." At six, I was babysitting. At twelve, I was standing between my siblings and chaos. I was not leading for trophies or applause. I was leading because somebody had to.

When my little brother scraped his knee, I cleaned it and wrapped it before he even thought to cry. When my sister was afraid at night, I made up stories that helped her fall asleep. When the fights at home got loud, I distracted the twins with games, shielding them from words too heavy for children's ears.

I became a mother long before I had children of my own. I became a mediator long before I had training in conflict resolution. I became a leader not because I was ready, but because life demanded it.

That early leadership was forged in fire. It was exhausting. It was unfair. But it built a strength in me that no classroom could teach. Today, when I lead teams or mentor young people, I bring that same steady presence. I know how to keep calm when tension rises. I know how to guide without dominating, how to listen even when I am the one holding authority. I learned empathy not from textbooks, but from holding the weight of four younger siblings on my small shoulders.

Sometimes people ask me how I remain calm when chaos breaks out in a meeting or when emotions flare in a mentoring circle. The truth is, I've been calming storms since I was a child. If I could keep my siblings safe in a living room filled with shouting, I can hold space for adults in a boardroom.

Basketball as Release

Basketball became my sanctuary. The sound of the ball bouncing against cracked pavement was like a drum calling me back to myself. Sweat poured down my face, knees scraped, lungs burning, but on that court, I wasn't the girl holding secrets. I was fast, fearless, untouchable.

Every layup, every rebound, was my rebellion against helplessness. When a defender shoved me, I pushed back harder. When I fell, I bounced up quicker. I didn't just play the game; I fought in it. And with every game, I was proving to myself that I was more than my circumstances.

There were days when the house was too heavy, when I felt like I couldn't take another scream, another slammed door. Those days, I would sprint to the nearest court, dribble until my hands ached, and shoot until the sun went down. The game gave me rhythm when life gave me noise.

Now, I see how that discipline and fire shaped me. Basketball taught me endurance. It showed me that pain can fuel progress, that persistence matters more than talent. It gave me a safe space to release anger, frustration, and sadness in a way that built me up instead of breaking me down.

Those lessons follow me into every speech I give, every project I lead, every risk I take in business. The same drive that pushed me to outrun the boys on the court pushes me now to outperform doubt and fear.

Finding My Voice

When my mother denied her drug use, my dad left. When silence sat heavier than arguments, I realized silence was dangerous. I learned that if I did not speak, the truth would never be told.

The first time I forced words out, they trembled, but they came anyway. I learned that even a shaky voice carried power. Over time, I discovered that telling the truth could change the outcome of a moment. It could shift the atmosphere.

I remember standing in the middle of the room, my heart racing, forcing myself to say out loud what everyone else was avoiding. My hands shook, my stomach churned, but my words cut through the fog. That moment taught me that courage is not about waiting for fear to leave. It is about speaking anyway.

Now, when I stand on a stage, I carry that same fire. My words are not polished just for applause. They are honest, shaped by storms, sharpened by survival. I know what it means to speak when your voice shakes, and that is why I can speak with clarity and conviction today.

That is why no one can silence me now. My voice was forged in chaos, tested in pain, and strengthened in truth. It was built in the storm, and it is weatherproof.

Looking back, I realize that the very storms meant to break me were teaching me how to stand. The chaos gave me instincts. The responsibility gave me strength. The game gave me fire. And my voice gave me freedom.

But storms do not vanish once you survive them. They return in new forms, carrying new lessons. To understand the woman I became, we must go back again, into the storm that followed, darker and louder than the first.

" " Latricia Ferris

You don't have to explain your peace to people who profit from your pain

Beyond the Storm **" "**

Towering Cumulus Cloud Formation

"Sometimes the calm before the storm is just your spirit catching its breath."

Affirmation: Even when I am being stretched, tested, or broken open, I am being prepared to rise.

A towering cumulus cloud does not look dangerous at first.
From a distance, it almost looks soft. Playful, even. Like something you would point to in the sky and name with a smile. That one looks like a dragon. That one looks like a heart.

But meteorologists know better. They know those rising clouds carry instability. The higher they climb, the more likely they are to become violent. Behind their fluffy white exterior is the makings of thunder, rainfall, and chaos.

That was my childhood.
Beautiful in moments. Chaotic underneath.

At fourteen, I was already carrying a weight most adults could not hold. I was working two jobs. I was raising siblings. And I was pretending every single day that I was okay.

I had traded my teenage years for survival.
Traded innocence for instinct.
Traded freedom for responsibility.

I thought I had lived through a lot already. But nothing prepared me for the night I found out my mother tried to take her own life.

It was the middle of the night.
The house was silent except for the creak of floorboards, the hum of the fridge, and the soft breath of my siblings sleeping in their rooms.

The phone rang. Sharp. Jarring. Like thunder cracking the stillness.
I waited for my mom to answer it. She always slept closest to the phone.

But it kept ringing.
And with every ring, my chest grew tighter.

I dragged myself out of bed, half-asleep, annoyed. "Hello?" I mumbled.

The voice on the other end was calm. Too calm.

"Is this Latricia?"

I straightened, my body already knowing something was wrong. "Yes?"

"This is Dr. Thomas with Denver Health. I am calling about your mother."

My breath stopped. The air thickened, pressing down on me.

"She is alive," he said quickly, as if he could hear the panic in my silence.
"But she was brought in tonight. She attempted suicide. She cut her wrist."

The walls tilted. The ground fell away. My body went cold.

"She is stable. She will be held for a psychiatric evaluation. She asked to speak with you."

And then I heard her voice.

Except it was not her voice. Not the one I grew up with. It was hollow. Detached.

I whispered, "Mommy... are you okay?"

For a split second, I hoped. I wanted her to say she loved us. That she was sorry. That she would fight.

Instead, she said words that split me open.

"I tried to kill myself because of you kids. I have made up my mind. I am choosing drugs over being your mother."

It was like lightning struck through my chest.
My hands shook. My throat closed.
But no sound came out.

The little girl inside me died that night.

I hung up and sat at the kitchen table, gripping the wood so tight my knuckles burned. The weight of her words pressed on me so heavily, I could not breathe.

She chose drugs over us.
She blamed us for her pain.
She blamed me.

And I was only fourteen.

I stared at the clock until sunrise, waiting for 5 a.m. so I could tell my grandma. When the sun finally came up, it did not feel like a new day. It felt like the sky itself had split open.

My grandma did what she always did. She held the family together like a thread in a worn quilt.
She confronted my mom when she returned from the hospital, her voice firm but steady.

"You cannot do this to these kids, Charlene," she said.

My mom apologized. She said she was fine now. She said she was sorry.

But apologies do not undo storms. They only try to explain the forecast.

For a short while, it looked like things were better. She cooked meals again. She laughed. She even tried to braid love back into the broken threads of our family.

I wanted to believe her. Part of me needed to. But deep down, I knew the storm was not gone. It had only shifted. It was quieter now, but heavier, darker, waiting for another way to break.

And then one afternoon, I came home from school and saw a man sitting on the couch.
He was maybe nineteen. Too young to be hanging around my mother, but too old for me.

She introduced him with a smile that did not feel right. Later, she told me, "He asked about you. Said you were pretty. I told him you were seventeen. Almost eighteen."

I froze.
I was fourteen.

The words did not feel like a compliment. They felt like a warning.
Something in my gut told me the air had shifted again.

At the time, I did not understand what was really happening. I thought maybe my mom just wanted me to meet someone nice. I told myself it was harmless. He smiled at me. He gave me attention. And after so many years of being overlooked, ignored, or silenced, that attention felt like love.

It would take me years to realize the truth. He was not simply interested in me. He had something my mother wanted. Drugs. And my access was part of the exchange.

At fourteen, I did not have the words for betrayal that deep. I only knew it felt like being handed over. Like my body was not fully mine anymore.

But in that moment, I did not see it. I thought I was being chosen. I thought I was being noticed.

And when you are starved for love long enough, even poison can taste like a feast.

When Love Breaks

Pause. Breathe. Reflect.

Some storms do not come with thunder or lightning. They come with silence. With words that cut deeper than any blade. With betrayals that do not leave bruises on your skin but instead settle into your chest, pressing down on your breath, making your heartbeat feel like a weight you can barely carry.

These storms are harder to see, harder to name, harder to explain. People ask, *"What happened?"* and you have no wound to point to, no visible scar to prove the pain. All you have is a memory that replays like a broken record. All you have is the heaviness that lingers long after the words were spoken, long after the betrayal has passed.

Take a moment. Allow yourself to go back—not to live there, but to visit honestly. What memory comes up first when you think of love breaking? Was it a moment with a parent? A friend? A partner? Was it the silence after an argument? Was it a sentence you cannot unhear?

Question 1: Has someone you loved ever said or done something that made you feel abandoned?

What did that moment sound like? Was it a slammed door? A phone ringing in the night? A voice telling you, *"It's your fault"*?

What did it feel like in your body? Did your stomach drop? Did your chest tighten? Did your hands shake? Did you feel heat rush through you or a coldness spread over your skin?

What did it look like around you? Were you sitting alone in a kitchen? Were you staring at a clock, waiting for daylight? Were you standing in a room full of people and still feeling invisible?

Abandonment does not always mean someone leaves physically. Sometimes they are still in the room, still in your life, but no longer choosing you. That absence is just as loud as footsteps walking away.

Question 2: What stories did you tell yourself at the time to survive?

Children and even adults often create stories to protect their hearts. Maybe you told yourself, *"It's not that bad."* Maybe you convinced yourself, *"They didn't mean it."* Maybe you accepted unsafe attention, just because it felt better than being ignored.

Think back. What did you tell yourself to keep going? Did you downplay what happened? Did you blame yourself? Did you quiet your own truth so you wouldn't have to feel the full weight of the betrayal?

Survival stories are powerful. They get us through the moment. But later, when the storm has passed, those same stories can keep us stuck. What stories have you carried long after the moment ended?

Question 3: Looking back now, what was the reality behind those moments?

With time and distance, you see things differently. You begin to realize what you could not name before. Maybe that "love" was actually manipulation. Maybe that "care" was actually control. Maybe that "attention" was actually an exchange you did not consent to.

What was the truth hiding underneath the story you told yourself? Did you want so badly to believe in love that you overlooked the harm? Did you confuse survival with affection?

And now—how do you feel about that? Not just about them, but about you. Can you look back with compassion for the younger version of yourself who only wanted to feel chosen, who only wanted to feel loved, who only wanted to feel safe?

This part of the reflection is not about blame. It is about truth. About permitting yourself to finally name what was really happening, even if it hurts to say it out loud.

Question 4: How has that storm shaped the way you love, trust, or protect yourself today?

Every storm leaves something behind. Some leave rubble. Some leave scars. Some leave lessons.

Think about how that betrayal—or that abandonment—still echoes in your relationships today. Do you guard your heart so tightly that no one can enter? Do you over-give, hoping love will not leave if you just give enough of yourself away? Do you silence your own needs to keep the peace?

What patterns can you trace back to that storm? Are there places where you still react as if the betrayal is happening all over again? Are there walls you've built that keep you safe but also keep love out?

And yet, notice the resilience. Notice how you survived. Notice how, even with the wound, you kept moving. Maybe you are still learning how to trust again. Maybe you are still learning how to love without losing yourself. That is okay. Healing is not linear.

Pause again. Breathe again. Reflect again.

This reflection is not about reopening wounds just to bleed. It is about looking honestly at the places where love broke you, and then recognizing the strength that grew in the cracks. You cannot control what was done to you. But you can choose what you do with it now.

You can choose to name the abandonment and still claim belonging.
You can choose to acknowledge the betrayal and still believe in love.

33

You can choose to see the poison for what it was and no longer mistake it for a feast.

This storm shaped you, but it does not define you. The love that broke you does not get the last word.

Journal Prompt:
Write a letter to the younger version of yourself who lived through that storm. Tell them what you wish someone had told you then. Offer them the compassion, the protection, and the truth they did not receive. And then, fold that letter. Keep it. Or burn it. Whatever feels like release.

Latricia Ferris

The same rain that tried to drown me taught me how to grow

Beyond the Storm

After the Storm: Lightning in My Bones

"The storm that tried to bury me only rooted me deeper. Now I rise with lightning in my bones and fire in my veins."

Affirmation: I am built to succeed. Betrayal may have lit the fire, but my persistence keeps it burning. I will never stop rising.

The night my mother chose drugs over us, I felt like the ground had been ripped out from under me. I could not count on her. I could not even count on the truth. And when I came home to see that man on the couch, smiling at me like I was a prize wrapped and waiting, I understood something deeper: no one was going to protect me but me.

That realization did not make me weak. It made me hungry. Hungry for stability. Hungry for independence. Hungry for a life that no one could snatch out of my hands. That hunger became my fire, my discipline, my reason to wake up when I wanted to quit.

I stopped looking for safety in other people and started building it inside myself. If I could not trust love to keep me steady, then I would trust my own grind. If I could not depend on promises, I would depend on persistence. I promised myself that no matter how young I was, no matter how much weight I had to carry, I would not break.

At fourteen, I was already working two jobs. My afternoons started at a daycare center, where I helped plan activities for students while they waited for their parents to pick them up. I loved it there. For a few hours each day, I felt like I was giving kids the childhood I was losing. I made up games, read stories, and poured myself into making their afternoons feel light.

There was one little boy who hated nap time. He would wiggle, complain, and cry until I finally sat down beside him. When I hummed softly and rubbed his back, his tiny body would finally relax. The trust in his eyes when he drifted off reminded me that even in my brokenness, I could still give someone else peace. That mattered to me. In those moments, I felt strong. I felt useful. I felt like maybe my pain had a purpose.

Sometimes, parents would pull me aside and thank me. They would tell me how much their child adored me, how their little ones ran to the door every morning because "Miss Latricia" would be there. I would smile politely, never telling them how much I needed those children just as much as they needed me. They thought I was mature for my age, but they didn't know the truth: I was surviving through their kids ' laughter.

When the daycare closed, I would catch the bus across town to Kmart. My shift was in the shoe department, restocking boxes and cleaning aisles that looked like a tornado had ripped through them. Customers tossed shoes everywhere, and I spent hours putting them back in place.

I hated that job. I hated the harsh fluorescent lights that buzzed overhead. I hated the sour smell of rubber soles that clung to my clothes even after I washed them. I hated how customers snapped their fingers, demanding sizes as if I were invisible until they needed me. My back ached from bending, my feet swelled from standing, and sometimes I caught myself nodding off on the bus ride home. But I kept showing up.

There were nights I would crawl into bed past midnight, too tired to eat dinner, only to wake up at six for school the next day. I learned how to push through exhaustion, how to hold my head up in class even when my eyelids fought to close. Teachers saw my grades and thought I had it all together. They had no idea I was carrying two jobs, four siblings, and a heart still bleeding from betrayal.

The daycare fed my spirit. Kmart tested my endurance. Together, they taught me balance. They showed me that sometimes you will love the work, sometimes you will hate it, but either way, you show up. And in showing up, you grow stronger.

That is when ambition was born in me. Not the kind you write down on a vision board, but the kind you tattoo into your spirit. The kind that says: I will never starve. I will never settle. I will figure it out. My ambition was not a dream—it was armor.

That hunger bled into everything I touched. I worked hard at school even when exhaustion threatened to drag me under, because I knew grades could become my ticket out. I learned how to stretch ten dollars into groceries for the week. I learned how to patch up shoes so they lasted another season. I learned how to fake a smile so my siblings wouldn't see my fear.

I picked up babysitting gigs on weekends, cleaned houses with my grandma, and hustled however I could. Every dollar I earned was proof that I could rely on myself. Every shift completed was another brick laid in the foundation of my independence. I was not waiting for anyone to rescue me. I was rescuing myself.

Years later, I made that truth permanent. On my right forearm, I had the words "Built to Succeed" inked into my skin.

That tattoo is not a decoration. It is a declaration. A scar turned into a statement. I remember the sting of the needle as the artist pressed the ink into my flesh. With every pass, I thought about the storms I had already survived. With every letter, I thought about the promises I had made to myself— that no matter how dark it got, I would rise.

When people ask me about it, I smile. I tell them it's my mantra, my reminder, my covenant. It is proof that the girl who once sat in silence after her mother's rejection did not disappear. She transformed. She fought. She built herself into a woman who would never fold.

Piece by piece, I was building a future I refused to let anyone take from me.

Looking back, I see now that betrayal gave me ambition. It showed me that waiting for someone else to hand me stability was a trap. I had to create it for myself. And that is exactly what I did.

When teachers doubted me, I worked harder. When peers underestimated me, I outpaced them. When exhaustion tried to crush me, I whispered to myself, "You only fail if you stop trying."

Even now, when storms come, I do not crumble. I pivot. I adjust. I move. Because that fourteen-year-old girl taught herself one thing above all else: persistence is power. Hustle is survival. Ambition is armor.

The storm that could have left me broken gave me lightning in my bones and hustle in my veins. It gave me a fire that never burns out. It made me relentless.

And just when I thought I could survive anything, another storm appeared. This one wore the face of love.

Latricia Ferris

Sometimes silence is the loudest chapter in your healing

Beyond the Storm

Storm Rages

Affirmation: Even when I am surrounded by chaos, I can stand in the center and see clearly.

Some storms do not begin with thunder. They rise quietly, slowly, and by the time you realize how dangerous they are, you are already inside them.

That is how it felt stepping into a relationship with someone I thought was nineteen.

At fourteen, I craved stability, attention, and care. He gave me all three, or at least that is how it seemed. He told me I was beautiful. He listened when I talked. He picked me up from school in his old-school car, music blasting like he was somebody. He handed me burned CDs of his music, little gifts wrapped in flattery, and I held onto them like proof that I mattered to someone.

The first time I walked into his house, the air hit me before anything else. It smelled of cologne so heavy it clung to the couches, the curtains, even the walls. The living room was arranged like a picture out of a hip-hop magazine: black leather couches, glass tables, and gold-framed mirrors catching every glint of light. On the surface, it looked polished, classy even. But if you paid attention, the signs were there. The blinds half-bent. The quick movements of people in and out. The way the outside screamed hood while the inside tried hard to dress it up.

I felt nervous walking in, but also grown. Out of place and yet important. Like I had stepped into a world bigger than mine, one that made me feel older than I was.

It did not take long before we crossed a line. We became intimate. I was nervous, but when he led, I followed. This time felt different than my first. My first had left me feeling used, dirty, and disgusted with myself. With him, I felt desired. For once, I felt like I was being handled with care. For a girl desperate to escape childhood pain, that feeling was intoxicating.

But care mixed with control is not love.

His house became a hangout spot. Music thumped so loud the walls seemed to shake. His friends gathered around card tables, gambling and shouting. Dice hit the hardwood, bottles of gin and tequila lined the counters, and cigarette smoke curled through the air. At first, I hated the taste of liquor. It burned, bitter and sharp. But I loved the way it made me feel. Warm. Bold. Free. Invincible. With a cup in my hand and laughter echoing around me, I could almost forget what waited at home.

That couch, that house, that world made me believe I belonged. But blurred boundaries always carry danger.

Around that same time, something shifted.

One afternoon, I stood on the balcony of our apartment with my cousin when two teenage boys walked by. One of them looked up at me, caramel-skinned with green eyes and a cocky smile. He wore a FUBU jersey, his bald fade sharp like he had just walked out of the barbershop.

"Hey, you in the gray shirt!" he called out, pointing straight at me.

I looked down, pretending to be unbothered. "You talking to me?"

"Yeah. You're cute. Come down here."

My cousin laughed, nudging me. "Girl, somebody likes you."

Heat rushed to my cheeks. I tried to roll my eyes, but the smile gave me away. I walked downstairs, nervous but curious. He introduced himself as Mike. His lines were ridiculous, his confidence almost too much, but something about him felt different. He felt younger, closer to my world, safer somehow.

Later, I would learn his real name was Aron. The fake name faded, but Aron stayed.

Not long after, the twenty-two-year-old went to jail. That relationship ended as suddenly as it had begun, but by then, my attention was already leaning toward Aron.

By fifteen, Aron and I were a couple. Our family moved into a triplex on 25th and Chester with my grandma, just blocks from where I had once learned about my mother's suicide attempt. Our unit sat at the front of the hill. Aron lived across the street in a flat-level triplex. Even when I was home, he was never far.

Life inside my grandma's apartment was crowded, loud, and raw. My grandma had her own room. My three brothers shared another. My sister and I claimed one, but instead of beds, we brought in two red couches and an entertainment center. The walls and even the ceiling were plastered with Word Up! posters of Usher, TLC, and Destiny's Child. Our space looked more like a hangout than a bedroom. Music blasted from our boombox daily, drowning out everything else like a shield.

Grandma's cooking filled the house with fried chicken, collard greens, and cornbread. Her cigarette smoke lingered in the hallways, mixing with bleach from her endless cleaning. My mom slept on the couch, her nights spent in front of the computer, chatting with men online, her voice low and distracted. She was still using.

It was chaos, but it was ours. And for the first time, with Aron by my side, I felt steady in the middle of it. He was protective and patient. Even months into our relationship, before our first kiss, he never rushed me. He made sure I was comfortable. That was new for me. That was peace.

But even in the eye of the storm, danger can circle close.

One night, when I was sixteen, I had been drinking with my sister and some of her friends. They passed around a bottle of gin. I hated gin, so I slipped away, stretching out on one of the red couches in our room. My pajamas were short, my body tired. Sleep pulled me under.

I woke to a hand on my thigh. His breath was hot on my face. His voice low, commanding: "You need to do what I say."

My body froze. My voice vanished. My heart slammed against my ribs. Every muscle screamed at me to fight, but all I could do was lie still. Here we go again, I thought.

Before he could go further, the door opened.

Aron stepped in. His eyes scanned the room, landed on me, then on him. Without a word, he understood. The tension snapped. He made sure that the man left. No questions. No interrogation. Just action.

Then he turned to me. "You okay?" he whispered.

That was all it took. My tears slipped out, hot against my cheeks. Relief washed over me in waves. Aron didn't demand details. He didn't make me relive it. He just wrapped me in his arms and let me breathe. That night, I left with him and slept at his house. For the first time in years, I closed my eyes without fear of what might happen while I slept.

The storm of that older relationship sharpened my instincts. It taught me that attention is not love, and blurred boundaries can turn dangerous fast. But meeting Aron showed me something new.

He taught me that safety was not a luxury. It was a necessity. That respect and patience could exist alongside love. That sometimes peace looks like falling asleep without checking the locks three times.

The eye of the storm does not mean the storm is gone. It means you are in the center, holding steady while the winds circle you. With Aron, I learned what it felt like to find calm even when the chaos had not ended.

That lesson was not easy. It came at a cost. But it planted a seed in me. A whisper that said: You can survive storms, but you can also grow from them.

In the Eye of the Storm
Take a deep breath. Settle yourself in.

Let your shoulders drop. Let your jaw unclench. Let your mind soften from the rush of the day.

Sometimes the most dangerous storms are not the ones that roar in with lightning and thunder. They are the quiet ones. The ones that come disguised as comfort, attention, or even love. They slip in slowly, and before you realize it, you are already in their eye, surrounded by winds you cannot control.

These storms are tricky. They make you feel chosen, seen, even protected at first. They whisper promises that sound like safety. But over time, they pull you under, asking you to trade your truth for their approval, your boundaries for their affection.

Take a moment now to reflect on your own storms.

When did attention feel like love to you?

Think back to the first time someone made you feel special. Did they call you beautiful, make you laugh, or make you feel like you mattered? Did their words or actions light something in you that you had been longing for?

Be honest—was that attention rooted in real care, or was it conditional? Did it last only as long as you did what they wanted? Did it feel like love in the moment, but leave you emptier afterward?

Write it down. Describe not just the moment but how it lived in your body—did your chest feel warm? Did your stomach drop later when the truth surfaced?

What blurred boundaries did you accept because you were desperate to feel chosen?

Storms often blur the line between safety and danger, love and control. Reflect on where you may have allowed boundaries to be crossed. Was it in a relationship where you accepted less than you deserved? Was it in a friendship where you gave more than you received? Was it in a job where you stayed silent when you should have spoken? Was it even with family, where you let loyalty keep you in unhealthy patterns?

Be gentle but honest. Write the moments you stayed when you should have walked away, or the times you silenced yourself to keep the peace. These confessions are not weakness—they are clarity.

Where did you find your center in the middle of chaos?

Even in the eye of the storm, there is stillness. Did you find yours in music, in prayer, in writing, in laughter with a friend, or in the arms of someone who truly cared for you?

Think of the anchors that kept you steady when everything around you felt unsteady. Who or what helped you remember that you were more than the storm you were in?

Write their names. Write those moments. Honor them.

What did the storm leave behind that surprised you?

Storms strip away illusions, but they also leave gifts. Maybe you discovered strength you didn't know you had. Maybe your instincts grew sharper. Maybe you gained awareness that allowed you to see red flags sooner. Maybe the storm gave you the courage to finally whisper—or shout—"never again."

Look for the treasures in your survival. They may be buried under pain, but they are there.

Grounding Practice

Close your eyes. Picture yourself standing in the center of a storm. The winds whip around you, the noise is deafening, but right where you are standing, there is calm. Inhale deeply. Exhale slowly. Whisper to yourself: *I can hold peace even in chaos. I can stand steady in the eye of the storm.*

Journal Prompt

Write about a time when you realized the attention you were receiving was not love. What did it feel like in the moment, and what did you learn about yourself afterward? End your writing by affirming what real love looks like for you today.

Remember: storms may shake you, but they also show you what can never be taken away. You are still here. You are still standing. And that means the storm lost.

66 **Latricia Ferris**

When the wind shiffted, so did I, and that's how I found my wings

Beyond the Storm

After the Storm: Shelter, I Built Myself

"Storms may bruise me, but they cannot break me. Every wound I carry has become a wall of strength I built myself."

Affirmation: I am my own shelter. I honor the storms I survived, and I trust the strength they built in me. I rise, not despite the storms, but because of them.

The storm with the older man could have left me hollow, but instead, it carved out space for something new. At fourteen, I mistook attention for love. At sixteen, I learned what safety could feel like. And in the middle of it all, I began to see that storms are not just endured, they are survived with lessons stitched into your skin.

Those lessons began to reshape me, piece by piece.

Learning to Read Energy

As a child, I learned to feel danger before it arrived. A slammed door. A shift in footsteps. A silence too heavy. By my teenage years, that intuition was second nature.

Chess sharpened that skill. My father taught me to play when I was young, and I carried those lessons into life. Every move mattered. Every mistake carried weight. My grandma's voice stayed with me, too: *never let your left hand know what your right hand is doing*. It was more than a saying. It was survival.

I learned to watch people with the focus of a meteorologist reading clouds. My intuition proved itself over and over, and I trusted it.

One afternoon at school, I noticed my sister's body stiffen before a boy even touched her. I grabbed her hand and pulled her away before the situation escalated. Years later, when a manager praised me to my face but I sensed resentment beneath the words, I documented every detail of our conversations. Quietly. Silently. Like a chess player moving pieces while the other side thought I was still deciding. When they later tried to twist my work behind my back, I had the proof to protect myself.

That moment confirmed what storms had taught me: my instincts were not paranoia. They were a strategy.

Shifting from Numbing to Healing

Alcohol had once been my escape. In the older man's world, drinking made me feel bold, free, even invincible. But when I found out I was pregnant at sixteen, I stopped instantly. My daughter became my reason to put the bottle down.

That choice saved me, but it did not erase the pain. Instead of alcohol, I found another coping mechanism: food. Emotional eating became my way of filling holes no one could see. Late nights of macaroni, fried food, or sweets felt like comfort, even though I knew deep down they were a cage.

At my heaviest, I weighed over 310 pounds. Yet when I looked in the mirror, I still saw the slim girl I once was. Like the movie *Shallow Hal*, my reflection lied to me, but inside I knew the truth. I carried my storms in my body, and each pound was proof of pain I had not faced.

Outwardly, I looked confident. I smiled. I kept moving. But inside, I felt worthless.

It took therapy to help me face the truth. To stop feeding my pain and start healing it. I remember one session where my therapist asked, *"What are you really hungry for?"* That question broke me open. I cried, not because I was hungry for food, but because I was starving for safety, love, and peace.

I lost over 100 pounds, not just from my body, but from my spirit. I learned that healing is not about hiding pain. It is about holding it, naming it, and then choosing differently.

Now, I drink only socially, and never when I am in pain. If the storms rise, I reflect. I pray. I meditate. I no longer numb myself. I listen.

Redefining Love

Being with Aron showed me what it meant to be cared for without conditions. After the chaos of the older man, his patience felt like water after fire. Even when he kissed me for the first time, he paused to ask if I was ready. That small act gave me something I had been missing for years: choice.

We built a life together, and when our marriage ended twenty years later, it could have torn us apart completely. But instead, it taught me something deeper. Boundaries are not walls to keep people out—they are guides to keep love whole.

Now, I take myself on dates. I buy myself flowers weekly. I remind myself that love begins with me. Because I cannot demand what I do not first give to myself.

Even in divorce, Aron and I learned to co-parent and eventually rebuild a friendship. That was the power of boundaries. That was survival grown into maturity.

Leadership Born in Storms

Survival made me a leader before I ever carried a title. But storms transformed that survival into advocacy.

Years later, I walked into a nonprofit space where youth on probation were gathered. Before the session began, I overheard the pastor speaking down to the students, his voice dripping with disrespect.

I felt the shift in the air instantly. The kids were shrinking. Shoulders hunched. Eyes down. I could not stay silent.

I stepped in and corrected the pastor with calm authority. Respect is not optional. Not for these young people. Not for anyone.

Afterward, I pulled the students aside. I looked them in the eyes and told them the truth: *you are worthy. You deserve respect no matter who is speaking to you. And even adults must live by that rule.*

That was survival turning into leadership. That was the voice I had once been denied, now speaking loud enough for a roomful of kids to hear.

And it was not the last time. I have spoken up in boardrooms when others stayed quiet. I have stopped conversations when leaders dismissed the voices of women or minorities. I have learned that storms give you courage, but they also give you responsibility.

Built to Succeed

On my right forearm, the words *Built to Succeed* are inked into my skin. That tattoo is not a decoration. It is testimony.

It is proof that every storm I walked through built me, not to break, but to rise.

I was reminded of that the first time I spoke publicly about my story. I stood in front of a high school class, invited to teach about entrepreneurship. A girl raised her hand and asked, "Why did you start your company?"

I gave the polished answer. The safe one. The room went flat. The girl lowered her head, and I felt something in me ignite.

I sat on the edge of the desk and told the truth. I spoke about my mother's addiction, about being a teen mom, about the storms that nearly destroyed me.

And the room shifted.

Phones were set down. Every eye lifted. Everybody leaned forward. It was like a golden string ran through each of us, connecting my story to their silent questions, their hidden battles. For the first time, I understood that my story was not shameful. It was an honor. It was survival turned into strategy.

That moment sealed it for me. I was not that scared little girl anymore. I was a woman carrying storms in her bones and lightning in her voice.

I was built to succeed.

Latricia Ferris

Your strength didn't come from what stayed. It came from what you survived

Beyond the Storm

The Breaking Storm

"Storms do not just pass by. They change the landscape forever."

Affirmation: Even when the sky splits open, I will not break. I will become the ground where new life takes root.

In middle school, I used to escape into the pages of C.S. Lewis. *The Chronicles of Narnia* was my favorite. There was something powerful about children stumbling through a wardrobe into a world where magic existed. Battles were fought there, but the battles had a purpose. Pain always carried meaning. Even war came with a prophecy.

That was not the world I lived in.

In my world, storms came without warning. Pain arrived without explanation. Survival had no prophecy, no promise.

When I found out I was pregnant, I longed for that wardrobe more than ever. A place where I could run, where none of it would be real. But Narnia wasn't coming. I had to find the magic inside myself.

My teenage dreams shattered quietly. Not with screams, but with an invisible weight pressing into my chest. It was the knowing: *everything is about to change.* I wasn't ready. I didn't know how to be a mother. But I knew, without question, I could not become my mother.

So I stopped drinking. Cold turkey. Alcohol had been my courage and my medicine. But this baby deserved better. I deserved better.

Fear slowly shifted into love. The first time I felt her flutter, it was like my soul exhaled.

My family, who had often scattered in different directions, gathered around me. My grandma was first, as always. She didn't wait for baby showers or hand-me-downs. She hit every thrift store in Denver with her sharp negotiating voice and her stubborn pride. She came home with bags full of baby clothes, bottles, blankets, and strollers. We weren't wealthy, but her love was extravagant.

My father took the news the hardest. For weeks, his voice was quiet. His presence felt distant. But eventually, something in him softened. He began calling himself "Papa," and his pride in me was wrapped up in that single word.

And Aron... he showed up too. He came to appointments. He held my hand. He didn't always know what to say, but his presence was steady. And in that season, presence was everything.

Pregnancy did not pause life. I still had to go to school, still had to walk through hallways with swollen ankles and morning sickness that came without warning. I would sit in class trying to focus, but waves of nausea hit like clockwork. Teachers sighed when I asked to leave. Classmates stared. My body felt like a spotlight, calling attention I didn't want.

One time, on the bus ride home, I couldn't hold it in. I threw up all over a man sitting next to me. His face twisted with disgust, and people laughed, covering their noses and making jokes. My cheeks burned with shame. I wanted to disappear, but there was no escape. That moment seared into

59

me how different my life had become. I wasn't just a teenager anymore. I was a pregnant teenager, and the world never let me forget it.

Friendships faded like smoke. Invitations stopped coming. Girls I had once laughed with now whispered behind my back. Even with the friends who stayed, the conversations changed. They talked about dances, games, and crushes. My world was appointments, swollen ankles, and saving money for diapers. I learned how to fake a smile and nod, then cry later in my room when no one was watching.

Still, I pressed forward. Books became my comfort again. I devoured pages, not just to pass the time but to remind myself that dreams were still possible. I clung to the idea of being a lawyer, of stepping into a life that would prove all the whispers wrong.

I left Kmart behind, but I wasn't free from the grind. My little sister and I both started working at Ward's. We stocked shelves together, walked the sales floor, and leaned on each other when our feet ached. Sometimes, in the middle of exhaustion, we cracked jokes to make the hours pass. Customers saw two teenage girls in uniforms, but they didn't see the storm beneath the surface. They didn't see that I was carrying both a baby and a future. They didn't see the fear I swallowed every time I caught someone whispering that I was "too young." Ward's wasn't glamorous, but each paycheck felt like another brick in the shelter I was building for my child.

At eight months pregnant, another storm cracked open. Aron had gone out one night, and I stayed home. The next morning, the news reached me that he had been robbed at gunpoint. The words hit me like a blow. My hands trembled.

My stomach knotted, not just with pregnancy but with fear. I wasn't there, but the image burned in my mind: the gun, the threat, the danger that could have taken him from me before our daughter was even born. When he walked in the next day, alive but shaken, I exhaled a breath I didn't realize I was holding. I wanted to collapse into his arms, but instead I held it in, swallowing fear the way I had been trained to all my life. Still, inside me the storm raged: *What if I had lost him? What if my daughter had never met her father?*

Then the sky cracked open.

It was November 6, 1999, at 10:30 a.m. when the contractions began. They rolled in like waves, pulling me under with every surge. The older women in my family told me to wait. "First babies take forever," they said. But the storm inside me kept building. Hours passed. My body trembled. The pain came sharp, then sharper still.

By the time I arrived at the hospital, I had been laboring for hours. Aron was by my side, his grip tight around my hand, whispering things I can't even remember now. My grandma prayed quietly under her breath.

And my mother... she decided this was her moment to teach me a lesson. In the 90s, pain medication during labor required parental consent. She refused to sign. She thought denying me an epidural would make me "learn."

The nurses saw my face twisted in pain. They saw the cruelty in hers. And eventually, they stepped in. After nearly eighteen hours of anguish, they gave me relief.

The storm shifted again.

The epidural numbed the sharp edges. The pain became rhythm. My body still labored, but I could breathe.

On November 7, 1999, at 10:31 a.m., after nearly twenty-four hours of labor, I gave birth to my daughter. Her cry filled the room like thunder. Not frightening. Powerful. That sound was not the end of my pain. It was the beginning of my transformation.

Motherhood is its own dimension. Nights stretch endlessly. Days blur. Your body no longer feels like your own, but your heart grows ten sizes. I learned to decode cries. To rock a baby on no sleep. To celebrate tiny victories as if they were gold medals. But life did not pause to let me catch up. School, work, family, all of it kept moving.

When I returned to school, they placed me at Florence Crittenton, a school designed for teen moms. For the first time, I didn't feel ashamed of being a young mother. I was surrounded by girls who understood. Teachers who didn't whisper judgment. For a while, it felt like shelter. But my mother hated it. She tried to re-enroll me in the public school system, and because it was mid-year, Aurora Central was where they sent me.

I remember walking in already feeling like an outsider. They placed me in a single-room class with a packet of busywork, like I wasn't worth the effort of real lessons. The teacher sat in the corner with headphones on. The hum of fluorescent lights filled the silence. Pages turned, but no one spoke. It felt less like school and more like punishment.

I hated it there. I missed my friends at Manual. I missed classrooms that buzzed with energy. Aurora Central felt like a holding cell.

So I left. I studied for the GED in secret. Only Tia knew. Every morning, I told people I was headed to school. But really, I was headed toward a future I was piecing together in the shadows.

And just when things began to feel steady, another storm rose.

It was a few days before Christmas when Tia burst through the door, her voice frantic. "Ma's behind the house with some strange man. She won't come home. She won't listen to me."

I was feeding my baby. I remember the warm weight of her against me, the smell of her soft hair, the quiet rhythm of her breathing. And in that moment, I chose her.

"No," I told Tia. "I'm not chasing Mama tonight."

Tia begged, but I was done. I have a daughter now. And I could not keep begging someone to choose us.

Mama didn't come home that night. Not the next day either.

Christmas morning came. Her chair sat empty. Her gifts were still wrapped. Granny baked pies. The twins sang silly Christmas songs. We laughed with knots in our stomachs.

By afternoon, the air grew heavy. We knew something was wrong. Granny called the police and filed a missing person report.

The next evening, the knock came. Two officers stood at the door, faces somber. They asked us to come identify a Jane Doe at the hospital.

My blood ran cold. The ride was silent except for the sound of our hearts breaking.

At the hospital, the woman in the bed barely looked human. Swollen. Bruised. Hair matted with blood. "This isn't her," we said. "It can't be her."

The officers explained that swelling changes everything. We needed to look for scars.

And that's when I saw it. The c-section scar. The toenail polish. Details only a daughter would know.

It was her.

My mother had been beaten nearly to death and left in the street.

The guilt struck me like lightning. What if I had gone that night? Could I have saved her?

But deep down, I knew. This storm had been gathering for years. And I could not save her from it.

All I could do was keep going.

When the Sky Breaks
Pause. Breathe. Reflect.

Close your eyes for a moment. Inhale deeply through your nose, hold it for three steady counts, then exhale slowly. Do it again, this time placing your hand over your heart. Feel the rise and fall of your chest. Feel the steady beat inside of you, the one that carried you through storms you thought might end you. That rhythm is proof: you are still here.

Some storms we cannot stop. They roll in, they strike, and we are left standing in the aftermath with nothing but our breath and our will. Sometimes they are loud, breaking us open in a single violent night. Other times, they are quiet, stretching across months or years, wearing us down little by little until one day we realize we have been surviving for far too long.

This chapter was one of those storms. Becoming a mother as a teenager. Watching my own mother disappear into her pain. Learning that love does not always protect, and sometimes the people we need most cannot choose us. These storms came one after another, and yet even in the breaking, I found pieces of myself. Storms do not only destroy; they reveal what is unshakable within us.

Take a moment to reflect:

1. When was a time in your life when everything changed overnight?
Did you see it coming, or did it strike like lightning out of a

clear sky? Sit with the memory for a moment. Where were you standing? Who was with you—or who wasn't? What sounds filled the air? Was it silence, or shouting, or the sound of your own heartbeat thundering in your ears? Write down those details. Naming them is the first step toward releasing them.

2. When the people you counted on did not show up, who or what gave you strength instead?
Maybe it was a grandmother who prayed over you. Maybe it was a child whose cry reminded you why you had to keep going. Maybe it was a friend who showed up with food, or simply sat with you in silence. Maybe it was a song, a scripture, a memory, or even your own reflection in the mirror. Take a moment to honor those sources of strength. Write their names. Describe their faces. Record their words. Hold onto them, because they are proof that you were never truly alone.

3. What guilt are you still carrying for storms that were never yours to control?
The "what ifs" and "if onlys" are heavy chains. What if I had left earlier? What if I had stayed? What if I had spoken up? What if I had stayed silent? These questions do not change the past. They only keep us bound to it. Write them down. Every single one. Let the ink carry the weight instead of your heart. Then look at your words and tell yourself: *This was never mine to hold.* You can whisper it, you can shout it, you can pray it—but you must let yourself release it.

4. How did that storm shape you?

Did it sharpen your strength, deepen your compassion, or push you to dream of something greater? Did it harden you, or did it soften you in places you didn't expect? Did it make you a protector, a provider, a truth-teller? Sometimes our hardest storms birth our greatest gifts. Write about the qualities in you that were born in the storm. Name them. Celebrate them. They are your inheritance from pain, your proof that nothing was wasted.

Remember: storms change the landscape, but they also carve rivers, grow forests, and make room for new life. What looks like destruction can become foundation. Sometimes the cracks left behind are the very places where light breaks through.

Journal Prompt

Think about a storm you've survived. Write it as if it were a weather report. Was it lightning-fast or slow and heavy like rain that would not stop? Describe the forecast, the damage, and then describe the aftermath. What was left standing when the sky cleared—and what new life began to grow in its place?

Grounding Practice

Place your hand over your heart again. Inhale and say silently, *I survived.*

Exhale and say, *I am still here.*
Repeat three times, until the truth settles into your bones.

Latricia Ferris

Don't Chase closure. Be the storm that ends the cycle

Beyond the Storm

70

After the Storm: Defying Gravity

"Storms do not just pass by. They change the landscape forever."

Affirmation: Even when the sky splits open, I will not break. I will become the ground where new life takes root.

The Storm's Aftermath

Becoming a mother at sixteen could have been the end of my story. Society had already written the script for me: failure, shame, statistics. They expected me to be another dropout, another girl buried by poverty and regret. But I refused to play the role they handed me.

Motherhood sharpened me. It made me honest. I never sugar-coated the truth for my children. I told them life could be brutal, that storms were real, but I also told them storms could be survived. I gave them manageable truths, hugs when they hurt, and space to dream without limits.

What I did not realize at first was that in giving them those things, I was healing parts of myself. Every time I told my children they were worthy, I was reminding the little girl inside me who had once doubted her worth. Every time I told them storms could be survived, I was reaffirming that my survival was proof.

And they thrived. My daughter built a thriving catering and baking business, shipping treats across the country. My son launched a photography and videography company, writes music, produces his own songs, and has even worked with Grammy-winning producers before the age of twenty. They chased their dreams not because life was easy, but because they saw that even in struggle, their mother never gave up. My love was the soil, but their strength was their own.

Taking in my bonus baby, J'honesty, was proof of how far I had come. For nine years, I was his full-time mom. He filled our home with laughter, tested my patience, and gave me new reasons to push forward. And when he returned to his biological mother after she turned her life around, I was not bitter. I was proud. Proud of her for choosing differently. Proud of him for growing strong. Proud of us for expanding love instead of shrinking it. Storms had taught me that love is not ownership; it is stewardship.

Rewriting Education

When schools tried to box me into watered-down programs, it only fueled me. Florence Crittenton gave me support, but Aurora Central gave me packets and neglect. The message was clear: you don't matter enough for our investment. But instead of letting that message define me, I let it light a fire in me.

I never earned a traditional college degree, but I built my own education piece by piece. Certificates from Harvard and Berkeley now hang on my wall. My true résumé is written in board seats, keynote speeches, global awards, and businesses I created from nothing. That path was not given to me—it was carved with determination, one choice at a time.

And now, I return to Florence Crittenton as an adult, standing in front of young mothers who feel invisible. I look into their eyes and remind them: you are not statistics. You are not ashamed. You are capable. You are worthy. You can rise. When I speak to them, I see shoulders lift, eyes sharpen, and hope stir again. That is pain turned into power in real time. What once felt like a dead end is now the very reason I can reach back and pull others forward.

Leadership and Forgiveness

Those early storms sharpened my sense of responsibility and discipline. I had already faced the worst kind of chaos at home, so corporate drama and professional challenges rarely shook me. I learned to put problems in perspective. A missed opportunity or a shift in leadership never felt like the end of the world, because I had already lived through storms that nearly ended mine.

The deepest shift came when I learned to forgive my mother. For years, I carried anger for her choices, her absence, her pain. I told myself forgiveness was impossible, that to forgive meant to excuse what she had done. But time—and survival—taught me differently.

It took seeing her in the ICU, frail and fighting for her life, for me to finally understand. She had loved me the only way she knew how. She had been storm-tossed herself, drowning in pain she never escaped. That truth permitted me to let go of bitterness and carry compassion instead.

Forgiveness did not erase the scars. But it freed me from being defined by them. Forgiveness was the moment the storm clouds parted, and I realized the sun was still shining.

Rising Beyond the Storm

I used to believe storms were designed to destroy me. Now I know they were shaping me. Every hardship became a lesson. Every loss carried a seed of resilience. Every crack in the foundation forced me to build stronger walls inside myself.

Today, I stand in rooms I once only dreamed of, speaking to crowds who lean in not just to hear my victories, but to understand the storms that forged them. When I tell my story, I see eyes widen, phones drop, and silence fill the space. It is not me they are seeing. It is reflected, reminding them that their storms can be transformed, too.

That is the power of survival turned into purpose. That is what it means to defy gravity.

And even now, with all I have built, I know the forecast is not finished. Storms still come. The difference is that I no longer fear them. I rise above them. I use their winds to lift me higher. What once threatened to break me now gives me wings.

My scars don't
whisper shame,
they testify to my
rise

Beyond the Storm

Storm Surge

"Some storms do not arrive all at once. They build in layers, stacking wave on top of wave, until you cannot tell which one knocked you down. You only know you are drowning."

Affirmation: Even when the surge rises higher than I can stand, I learn how to swim.

The first storm came in the form of truth I was never meant to hear. I was twelve years old when the phone rang, and on the other end was a man named Ricky. His voice was rough, heavy, and certain. "I'm your dad," he said.

The words shattered me before I even knew why. My hand gripped the receiver so tight it left my fingers numb. My stomach dropped, and my throat closed like it was trying to keep the words from sinking in. Before I could even speak, Chester, my father, who had raised me, the man I called Daddy, snatched the phone from my hand. His eyes burned, his jaw tight. He listened for a second, his face darkening, then slammed the call shut.

"You're smart, right?" he asked me, his voice sharp but steady. I nodded, afraid of what would come next. "That man may be your biological father, but I'm your real dad. Don't forget that."

I swallowed the words whole, but they cut me all the way down. My real dad? My biological dad? Which was I supposed to believe? The man who raised me, or the man who called me from the shadows of a life I didn't know? My chest ached like someone had knocked the wind out of me, and the silence that followed felt louder than anything I'd ever heard.

I wanted to scream. I wanted to ask why, how, and when. But the questions burned in me without a place to go. No one around me wanted to answer them. So, I learned to carry them. To bury them. To walk through the days pretending my world hadn't cracked in half. At twelve years old, I stopped asking who I was because I was terrified of the answer.

Years passed, and I tucked the memory away like an old scar. But scars itch. They burn. They remind you they're still there even when you try to forget. By the time I was nineteen, I told myself it didn't matter anymore. Chester was the one who raised me. He was the one who stayed. I thought that was enough.

Then Fatso, aka Melvin Jr., my cousin, came to spend the summer with me in Colorado. We laughed, we shared secrets, and even had moments that felt like freedom. That summer, we even met Lil Wayne. Life felt almost light again. But storms don't let you stay in the sun for long.

One night, Fatso sat me down. His eyes were serious in a way that scared me. He told me he had found a letter from my mom to his father, and a reply from his father back to her. Their words hinted at what I had tried to bury: that I did, in fact, have another biological dad. But instead of it being Ricky, it might have been his brother Melvin all along. Chester's silence wasn't clarity; it was protection. Or maybe it was denial. Fatso looked at me hard and said, "I think you're my sister."

The ground dropped beneath me again. My stomach clenched, and the air felt thin. I was confused, angry, hurt, and worst of all, I felt invisible. Who was I really? My identity shifted like sand, and no matter how I stood, I couldn't find balance. I carried that weight in silence, because what else could I do? My family was already drowning in their own storms. To speak it aloud would have been another wave to pull us all under.

And then Fatso was gone. Gunned down weeks later in Texas. At his funeral, I stood with Dana and the rest of his family, surrounded by grief so heavy it stole the air from the room. I wanted to scream the truth he had told me, to confess that I was carrying his secret too. But I stayed silent. I buried my questions with him, my pain tucked under my ribs like broken glass. For the first time, I realized silence wasn't just survival, it was suffocation. And yet I did it anyway.

That silence followed me into love. Years later, I found myself standing in a different storm, one that looked familiar in the worst way. This time it wasn't about who my father was. It was about the man I loved, the father of my children, and the secrets he kept until they drowned me.

I was in the living room, ironing clothes, the scent of lemon candles filling the air. Our two-bedroom house felt small but steady. The TV hummed in the corner. Danajha, only four years old, sang to her dolls in the next room. For a moment, life felt quiet, almost safe. Then it happened, the same way it had when I was twelve. That knowing. That sharp, gut-deep truth landed on my chest like a weight I couldn't push off.

"You have another baby," I said to Aron. My voice was steady, but inside I was unraveling. I didn't yell. I didn't cry. I just said it.

For a second, his face betrayed him. Then his mouth caught up with a lie. "No. I don't." But I already knew. Later, when the truth spilled out, it came with a name. Anthony. A baby boy.

That night, I lay awake listening to the creaks in the walls, the sigh of the house, the sound of my daughter's soft breaths. I stared at the ceiling and wondered how long I had been asleep in my own life.

But the storm wasn't done. It never was. Another wave rose at the end of my pregnancy with our son. My ankles were swollen, my back aching, my belly stretched so tight it felt like the moon itself. We were having a small gathering, neighbors, cousins, laughter, and the smell of fried food in the air. Amauri's mother was there. She smiled like she belonged in the room. Later, her cousin leaned in close and whispered, "You know she's pregnant, right?"

I froze. "Pregnant by who?"

Her eyes didn't move. "By him."

The room didn't stop moving, but I did. Laughter kept ringing, plates kept clinking, but the floor tilted beneath my feet. Another woman. Another baby. My hands pressed against my belly, feeling my son roll inside me. Two women are carrying the same man's child at the same time. I smiled so I wouldn't break, but inside, I was drowning.

And just when I thought I couldn't take another wave, I found a photograph. I was cleaning out the SUV, lifting a tote, when I saw it: soft baby cheeks, bright eyes, and on the back, carefully written: Jakhi Aron Walker. My hands shook. My knees buckled. Another child. Another truth I had never been given. And the name, Aron. The same as my son. The one I had bent my dreams around, naming him junior to tie father and son together forever. That bond, that sacred gift, was handed out again like it didn't matter.

The betrayal burned deep, but what hurt most was how familiar it felt. It echoed the same wound I had carried since I was twelve years old, when I learned the man, I thought was my father might not be. Once again, I was left questioning who I was, what was real, and why truth always came to me like thunder without warning.

Betrayal doesn't just break your trust. It breaks your reflection. It makes you question your worth, your choices, even your voice. And yet, just like when I was twelve, I swallowed the pain and stood back up. Because survival was the only option I had ever known.

These storms stripped me raw, but they also carved out something unshakable in me. I was still here. Battered, scarred, but standing. And each wave, no matter how high, was teaching me one thing: I could learn to swim even when the water tried to pull me under.

When the Waves Keep Coming
Pause. Breathe. Reflect.

When Truth Shakes Identity

Some storms are not about weathering the outside world. They are about surviving the truths that shake the foundation of who we are. Sometimes the storm is a revelation about family. Sometimes it is betrayal from a partner or friend. And sometimes it is silence—the unanswered questions that echo louder than any words could.

Storms like these can leave us feeling unmoored, unsure of who we are or where we belong. They can make the ground beneath us feel unsteady, even when everything on the surface looks calm.

Take a moment to reflect:

1. **Have you ever faced a truth that made you question your identity or belonging?**
   (How did it feel in your body? Did your chest tighten, your stomach clench, your thoughts scatter?)

2. **Have you ever discovered something that changed the way you saw someone you loved?**
   (Did it break your trust, shift your perspective, or force you to carry silence where words should have been?)

3. **What storms of betrayal have you had to survive?**
   (How did you respond—with anger, with silence, with forgiveness, or by building walls around your heart?)

4. **How do you carry unanswered questions in your life?**
   (Do they still ache like fresh wounds, or have you learned to live with them as part of your story?)

5. **What anchors you when your sense of identity feels shaken?**
   (Faith, family, creativity, resilience? What keeps you standing when you feel like you're drifting?)

These are not questions with quick or easy answers. They are questions that deserve time, honesty, and gentleness with yourself.

Journal Prompt: Write about a time when you discovered something that changed how you saw yourself or someone you loved. Begin with the moment itself—what you heard, saw, or felt in your body. Then explore how you carried it: Did you bury it in silence, did you share it, or did it shape your choices in ways you only realized later? Finally, reflect on what that storm taught you about your strength and what you want to carry forward.

Grounding Reminder

When betrayal or uncertainty rises like a storm, pause and remind yourself: *I am more than what was hidden from me. I am more than the choices of others. I am still here, and I am becoming.*

If it feels overwhelming, take three grounding breaths. With each inhale, say silently: *I am here.* With each exhale, say: *I am whole.* Let the rhythm remind you that storms may shake you, but they cannot erase you.

Latricia Ferris

Peace hits different when you had to fight for it

Beyond the Storm

86

After the Storm: Steady Rain

"Rain does not apologize for falling. It nourishes even as it soaks the earth. "

Affirmation: I choose to let the steady rain of my lessons water new growth in me and in others.

From Betrayal to Belonging

When the storm of betrayal first struck, it nearly drowned me. My chest ached with questions I could not answer, and my heart felt like it was carrying bricks instead of blood. But in time, I began to see something powerful. The children born from Aron's choices were not storms; they were blessings. They were not reminders of what I lost, but living proof that love can expand even through pain.

I never took my hurt out on those children. I refused to let betrayal define how I loved. Over the years, I attended their graduations. I sang at their birthdays. They slept in my home, laughed at my table, and became my forever family. Even though their father and I divorced long ago, our bond never broke. They are mine, and I am theirs. Their laughter reminded me that joy could still exist in places touched by betrayal. Their hugs proved that love can thrive even where trust once shattered.

Looking back, I realize where I learned that lesson. From my own father. Chester may not have been my biological father, but he raised me as his own, fully aware I might not share his blood. He never let that change his love for me. He showed up for me, fought for me, claimed me. That choice taught me what true fatherhood and true love look like. It taught me that DNA does not define family; commitment does.

That revelation shaped the way I love. It gave me the strength to extend the same unconditional love to children who weren't born to me. That is the steady rain. Betrayal taught me to hold the innocence of children above the brokenness of adults. It taught me to create belonging where others might expect bitterness. Love was no longer fragile; it was rooted, tested, and strong.

Healing What Cannot Be Answered

I still do not know the full truth about my biological father. That uncertainty is a storm that never fully clears. Some nights I would lie awake, staring at the ceiling, wondering if the silence around me was hiding more truths. But instead of letting it define me, I chose to use it as fuel.

When I mentor young people who feel invisible, I remember what it was like to carry unanswered questions. I remember what silence feels like, and I refuse to leave them in it. I look them in the eyes and say, "You belong. You matter. You are not defined by the pieces you don't know."

That is how I transformed pain into power. By giving to others what I once needed most. By creating certainty where I once had none. By being the steady voice when mine once trembled.

Redefining Strength

Storms taught me that strength isn't about pretending everything is fine. It's about standing in the rain and learning to breathe anyway. I had to unlearn the performance of perfection and embrace the honesty of survival. Strength looked like showing up to work with tears dried, but the heart was still aching. Strength looked like cooking dinner with nothing in the fridge, but making it feel like a feast. Strength looked like sitting across from my children and telling them hard truths in words they could hold.

When my marriage broke apart, I didn't hide it from my children. I told them the truth in a way they could carry. I let them see my tears, but I also let them see me rise. I showed them that storms can break you open without breaking you apart. I showed them that steady rain brings growth, even when skies are gray.

The Steady Rain of Hope

The rain in my life no longer feels like punishment. It feels like rhythm. It feels like something I can trust. Each drop carries a lesson, and when I let those lessons soak in, they grow into tools I use to lead, to love, to mentor, to speak.

When I stand in front of students or young mothers, I tell the truth. I share not only the victories, but the betrayals, the heartbreaks, the uncertainty. Because the rain only nourishes when we let it fall freely. My story waters theirs, reminding them that they, too, can rise.

The steady rain of my life is not about survival anymore. It is about growth. It is about creating shelter for others while the storm still rages outside. Hope is not a distant rainbow, it is the steady rain that teaches us how to live in the storm without losing ourselves.

Practical Lessons from the Rain

1. Betrayal does not define the way you love. (You get to choose how you show up for the innocent.)

2. Family is not limited to DNA. (Commitment is the real bloodline.)

3. Unanswered questions do not erase your worth. (You are still whole, even when you do not have every answer.)

4. Strength is not about never breaking down. (It's about rising again and again until standing feels natural.)

5. Healing happens in layers, like steady rain. (Give yourself time to soak, to grow, to bloom.)

The storms of my past carved valleys in me. The steady rain of healing filled them with rivers that now flow outward, carrying life to others. I do not waste my storms. I let them water the world. My steady rain is not the end of the storm. It is the gift that follows.

Standing in the Rain with Others

The most powerful lesson the steady rain taught me is that healing is not meant to be hoarded. It is meant to overflow.

I take the lessons I have lived through and hand them out like umbrellas in a storm. Not because I can stop the rain for others, but because I can help them find shelter long enough to catch their breath.

When I walk into rooms full of young people, mothers, or leaders carrying invisible weights, I see myself in them.

I know the silence of unanswered questions. I know the sting of betrayal that lingers in the body. I know the exhaustion

of carrying more than your share. And so I speak with transparency. I tell the truth of my storms not as tragedies, but

as testimonies. Because when one person stands in the rain unashamed, it permits others to stop hiding their storms, too.

Building Beyond the Storms

Every storm in my life gave me something: discipline, empathy, resilience, or perspective. I could have let them bury me, but instead I used them as bricks. Today, those bricks form the foundation of the businesses I have built, the speeches I give, and the mentorship programs I lead. The steady rain is what keeps me grounded. It reminds me not to chase perfection but to honor progress. To celebrate the small steps as much as the milestones.

That is why, even now, I do not run from the forecast. I know rain will come again. But this time, I will not fear it.

I will let it fall, let it water the seeds of dreams I continue to plant, and let it wash away anything that no longer serves me.

This is how I live beyond the storm with courage, compassion, and an unshakable belief that no matter what falls, I will rise.

Latricia Ferris

The storm tested me, but my spirit refused to break

Beyond the Storm

94

Shattered Skies

"The sky does not ask permission before it breaks, but even shattered skies make room for light ."

Affirmation: Even when the storm shatters my body, my spirit refuses to break.

The townhome looked like a dollhouse from the outside, with two neat windows, a door framed by a small porch, and a sloped roof that almost looked like something from a storybook. It was the kind of house people passed by without a second glance, but to me,
it represented a new beginning. Aron and I had just been married. We had stood in the Denver Botanic Gardens with flowers surrounding us, promising to choose each other, even though our lives had already been marked by storms. I thought marriage
would be the calm after chaos, the moment when everything finally settled. But storms don't wait for permission. They gather quietly, sometimes disguised as ordinary days, and then they break. And when they break, they shatter everything you thought
was safe.

It started with a knock at the door. A man stood there, saying he was the previous tenant. His face was worn, his clothes loose, and his voice carried a kind of urgency. He said he had

left something in the attic, something he needed to retrieve. At first, it seemed harmless, but something in my chest tightened. We called the landlord, and her response shifted the air
in the room. She explained that the tenant had been evicted for running a meth lab. The attic above our heads had once been a place of poison. My stomach dropped. My children's bedrooms were only feet away, their lungs fragile, their laughter echoing in the very house that might still hold remnants of danger. Aron and I looked at each other, and without words, we knew: we had to check for ourselves.

The attic was dim, the air stale and heavy. Dust clung to the beams like cobwebs of the past. A weak light bulb flickered, barely illuminating the broken-down boxes scattered across the wooden planks. Aron moved ahead of me, his body tense, his footsteps careful on the beams that groaned with each step. I followed, my eyes scanning the space, my chest tight. I wasn't thinking about danger for myself. I was thinking about what could still be hidden here that might hurt our kids.

Then it happened. One flattened box lay on the floorboards, covering a hole I could not see. The moment my weight pressed down, the cardboard collapsed. Time slowed. There was a crack, the groan of wood giving way, a rush of air that lifted my hair from my face. For a heartbeat, it was as if I hung suspended, the world tilting beneath me. Then I fell.

I crashed feet-first into the bedroom below. The sound was violent, a splintering of boards, a thud that rattled the walls. The breath was knocked from my chest. For a moment, there was no pain, just silence. I opened my eyes to see the jagged hole above, daylight spilling through like cruel evidence. I tried to move. Nothing. My body did not obey. My mind screamed: I am paralyzed. My life is over.

Aron's face appeared above me, pale, eyes wide with terror. His mouth opened, but words refused him. His hands trembled as he grabbed the phone, but fear strangled him. He couldn't even tell them our address. Lying there, shattered, I found my voice. I gave 911 the address, steady though my body screamed. Even in that moment, I had to be the strong one.

The sirens came quickly. Red and blue lights painted the windows. Paramedics lifted me onto a stretcher, strapping me in place. That was when the pain came. It roared through me like fire, searing from my hips to the middle of my back, stealing my breath. My throat burned as I cried out, my voice raw. Aron followed close, his hands shaking, his eyes refusing to leave me. I stared at the ceiling of the ambulance, the fluorescent lights passing in quick rhythm, and thought of my children.

The hospital became my storm shelter, but it did not feel safe. The walls were white but felt gray, drained of warmth. Machines beeped in rhythm, steady and cold, while fluorescent lights flickered above me without mercy. Sleep was a stranger. Each night, I drifted between consciousness and pain, hearing the groans of patients in nearby beds. The sound of a nurse's shoes squeaking on linoleum became my midnight lullaby. I watched shadows stretch across the ceiling and wondered if this would be the rest of my life, waiting, hurting, breathing, but not living.

Family came and went, their visits like gusts of wind in the middle of a storm. Some stood by me faithfully, speaking words of encouragement, holding my hand. Others disappeared, unable to face my fragility. That absence spoke louder than words. I learned in those days who could stand in storms with me and who could not.

Aron stayed. His presence was not perfect; we had our wounds, our unfinished arguments, but he stayed. He sat in the chair by my bed, eyes half-closed but unwilling to sleep. He read the monitors even though he didn't understand them. When I cried, he didn't try to fix it; he just held my hand tighter. That steadiness etched itself into me. I had once doubted his love,
but here he was, carrying me when I could not carry myself.

Recovery at home was a battlefield of humility. The brace was suffocating, stiff against my ribs, and the walker felt like chains more than freedom. Aron had to lift me from the bed, steady me on the toilet, and hold me in the tub. Every task became a reminder of what I had lost. Independence had been my pride. Now, dependence humbled me in ways words can't capture. I cried when my daughter brushed my hair, because her small hands were doing what mine should have. I cried when my son pushed his toys toward me, waiting for me to play, while my body screamed in protest at even the smallest movement.

Depression crept in silently. Pain pills dulled the ache but blurred the edges of reality. Days bled together, each one a mirror of the last. I stared at my scar and hated it. The jagged line running from my shoulder blades to my hip was a constant reminder that I was broken, less than whole. I avoided mirrors, avoided cameras, avoided myself. I whispered prayers into the silence: "Why me? Haven't I survived enough already?" Some nights, no answer came. Other nights, I felt a whisper deep in my spirit: "Because you can rise."

That whisper became my anchor. They told me I would never walk the same again, that my body would never recover. I made a decision: I would prove them wrong. After my third surgery, strapped into the brace, weak and trembling, I begged the nurse to let me stand. She shook her head, warning that it was too soon, but I refused to surrender. With help on both sides, I pushed through the fire in my spine. My legs quivered, tears blurred my vision, but I lifted. One foot forward. Just one. It felt like a marathon compressed into a single step. Then I sat back down, my body drenched in pain, but my spirit alight. That step was proof. Proof that I could overcome, even if the road was long.

The months that followed were marked by small victories. Eight months later, I managed the walker. A year later, I stood in the kitchen long enough to cook again, my children cheering as if I had crossed a finish line. The first time I tucked them into bed without collapsing, I cried silent tears of gratitude. The day I finally turned the key in the ignition and drove again, freedom tasted like oxygen. These weren't just milestones. They were miracles stitched into ordinary life.

The scar I once despised began to change in my eyes. At first, I avoided it, hated its jaggedness. But slowly, I began to trace it with my fingers, not as ruin but as testimony. That scar was proof that the sky could shatter, that bones could break, but the will to rise would remain. My body carried metal, screws, and pain, but it also carried resilience. My scar wasn't shameful. It was sacred.

Breaking my back taught me to respect the fragility of the

human body. It taught me to value health in ways I never had. It taught me resilience, that storms can strip away everything, but cannot erase the will to fight. It deepened my faith. Even when the nights were silent, even when the prayers felt unanswered, I knew Yahweh was there. His presence was not in
the absence of storms, but in the strength to survive them.

The sky had shattered above me. But in the pieces, I found light. I was not paralyzed. I was not erased. I was still here. Breathing. Fighting. Becoming. And the storm that tried to break me became the storm that built me stronger than I had ever been.

Recovery was not a straight line. It was a winding road, full of detours, setbacks, and days where hope seemed to vanish. There were mornings when I woke up determined to push further, and there were mornings when I could barely lift my head from the pillow.

Pain was constant, sometimes sharp like knives, other times dull like heavy stones pressing into my spine. It became a companion I had to learn to live with, even when it whispered lies that I was broken beyond repair.

Nighttime was the hardest. When the house grew quiet and the lights dimmed, the storm inside me grew loud. I would lie awake, my body heavy with the brace, listening to the hum of the refrigerator, the faint ticking of the clock, and the muffled sounds of my children breathing in their sleep. I wanted so badly to tiptoe into their rooms, to scoop them up into my arms, to sway with them in the moonlight the way I once had. Instead, I stared at the ceiling and let silent tears stream down my face. I felt robbed of motherhood, of intimacy, of freedom. I wrestled with shame. Was I enough if I couldn't move? If I couldn't provide? If I couldn't be the mother I had once promised myself I'd be?

Aron carried more than my weight during those years. He carried the household, the bills, the endless list of things I once managed without thought. I didn't always trust him before, but in my weakness, I saw a version of him I hadn't seen before. He showed patience, care, and even tenderness. He brushed my hair without complaint, helped me adjust pillows at 2 a.m., and held me steady when my legs trembled with effort. I didn't forget his failures, but I also couldn't deny his presence. It was humbling, and it softened some of the anger I carried. Sometimes storms force people to show who they really are. He showed up.

My children became my mirrors. My daughter's compassion reflected to me the love I had poured into her. She learned to nurture by watching me, and though it hurt to see her step into that role so young, it also reminded me that my love wasn't wasted. My son, too young to understand, became my reason to keep trying. His small hands tugging at me, his innocent requests for "Mama, up," kept me fighting for the day I could say yes again.

There was a night when despair nearly swallowed me whole. I had tried to move too much that day, stubborn in my pursuit of progress. The pain was unbearable. My body refused to cooperate, and my spirit cracked under the weight of it all. I remember sitting in the bathroom, the tiles cold under my feet, the walls closing in. I whispered, "I can't do this anymore." For a moment, I believed it. For a moment, I considered giving up. But then I heard my daughter's laughter from the other room, light and unbroken, and it pulled me back. Her joy reminded me why I had to keep

going. Storms can make you forget your
strength, but love has a way of reminding you.

Faith became both my anchor and my question. I argued
with Yahweh in those days. I asked why He allowed me to
fall, why He let my body be broken when I had already
survived so much. But I also clung to Him, because where
else could I go? I prayed through tears, sang hymns under
my breath, and let Scripture speak to me in ways it never had
before. "Though I walk through the valley of the shadow of
death, I will fear no evil." I repeated those words like oxygen.
Slowly, I began to see that faith was not about avoiding
storms but enduring them with the assurance that I was not
alone.

The turning point wasn't one dramatic event; it was a series
of small moments stitched together like patches on a quilt.
One day, I stood longer than before. Another day, I walked a
few extra steps. Some days, progress felt invisible, but over
time, it became undeniable. The scar on my back, which I
once hated, began to change meaning. Instead of seeing it as
ugliness, I began to see it as art, a masterpiece of survival. I
touched it with reverence, tracing its jagged edges as a
reminder that I was still here.

When I finally walked without the brace, my children
clapped and cheered like I had won a gold medal. Their joy
was pure, unfiltered, and it lifted me higher than any
medicine ever could. For them, it wasn't about how fast or
how far I walked. It was about the fact that Mama was
standing again. For me, it was proof that broken does not
mean finished.

Years later, I still carry the metal in my spine, and some days the pain lingers like a shadow. But the lessons that the storm taught me never fade. My body may have been shattered, but my spirit grew unshakable. Storms strip away illusions, but they also reveal truths we wouldn't see otherwise. The truth I carry is this: I am resilient. I am proof. I am not defined by the breaks, but by the ways I rise again.

The skies shattered, but even in the fragments, the light found me. And I chose to let it in.

As weeks stretched into months, I began to realize that recovery was not simply about my body; it was about my identity. I had always been the strong one, the caretaker, the leader. Now, I had to relearn what strength meant. It no longer looked like carrying everyone else on my shoulders. Sometimes, strength looked like asking for help, or admitting I couldn't do it alone.

Breaking my back was not just a physical injury. It was an emotional earthquake, a spiritual reckoning, a test of everything I thought I knew about myself. It stripped me bare, but it also rebuilt me from the inside out. I learned that strength is not the absence of weakness; it is the decision to rise again despite it. I learned that love is not proven in perfect words but in showing up, day after day, even when it's hard. And I learned that faith is not about being spared from the storm, but about finding purpose in the rain.

The sky had shattered above me, but I was not destroyed. I was transformed. And though I still carry the metal in my spine and the ache in my bones, I also carry the unshakable truth that storms do not define me. How I rise from them does.

Rainy Days
Pause. Breathe. Reflect.

Pause. Breathe. Feel the ground beneath you. Notice the rhythm of your breath—steady, alive, unstoppable.

Even in your hardest moments, even in the storms that shattered you, this truth remains: you are still here.

Some storms arrive in the body, taking away independence, movement, and confidence. They strip us down to the core,

forcing us to ask: Am I still worthy when I cannot do what I once could? Am I still me when I need others to carry me?

These questions are painful, but they are holy. They point us back to the truth that our worth is not tied to

our strength, but to our survival. Our scars do not mark us as ruined—they testify that we endured.

Take a moment to reflect:

1. **Have you faced a moment when your body or circumstances left you powerless?**

(How did your heart respond? Did you feel fear, anger, or grief? How long did it take before you could see even a sliver of strength in yourself?)

2. Who showed up for you when you were at your most vulnerable?

(Did their presence surprise you? Did their care change the way you saw them or yourself?)

3. What scars, seen or unseen, do you carry that remind you of survival?

(Do you hide them in shame, or can you begin to see them as proof of strength?)

4. How have storms reshaped the way you see yourself?

(Did they reveal weakness, or did they uncover resilience you did not know was inside you?)

Now, ground yourself in this truth: storms may shatter the body, but they cannot break the spirit unless you let them.

Even when skies split open, light still filters through the cracks.

Close your eyes for a moment. Imagine yourself lying beneath a broken sky. The clouds are torn. The light is dim.

You feel small and heavy, unsure if you can rise. Now imagine yourself slowly standing, scarred but upright.

The air is the same, but you are different. Stronger. Wiser. Whole in a new way.

✧ Journal Prompt

Write about a time when life shattered something you depended on, your body, a relationship, or your sense of safety. What did that storm take from you? What did it leave behind? Describe how your scars, physical or emotional, might be reframed not as symbols of loss, but as living proof that you survived.

Remember this: scars are not shame. They are sacred reminders. You are not broken. You are proof.

Forgiveness isn't weakness, it's emotional graduation

Beyond the Storm

After the Storm: Strength Forged in Recovery

Affirmation: I have the power to endure, to rise, and to transform my pain into purpose.

The months after breaking my back felt like standing in front of a mirror with no choice but to face myself. My body was fragile, my spirit restless, and everything in me wanted to escape the pain. I couldn't. There was no exit door, no shortcut, no fast-forward button to skip the suffering. The only way forward was through. Day after day, I had to make a decision: would I lie down and let life bury me, or would I fight to move, inch by inch, until strength returned?

I learned perseverance in real time when I had to teach my body how to walk again. It wasn't glamorous. It wasn't a motivational video clip with uplifting music in the background. It was sweat pooling down my back as I tried to lift one leg off the ground. It was tears burning my eyes when pain shot through me so sharply, I thought I might faint. It was the embarrassment of needing help to do things I once did without a second thought, getting dressed, stepping into the shower, and bending to pick something up off the floor.

Every moment became a test of willpower, and every small victory carried the weight of a miracle.

There were days I questioned whether I would ever be the same again. Nights where I lay awake, staring at the ceiling, wondering how a single fall had rewritten my entire future. But then there were moments, tiny, almost invisible moments, where progress came. The first time I stood for more than a few seconds without collapsing. The first time I took three steps in a row without someone holding me. The first time I laughed at my own clumsy movements instead of crying. Perseverance wasn't loud; it whispered to me through each small milestone: Keep going. This matters.

I realized perseverance is not built in giant leaps. It's built in the stubbornness to keep moving when nobody is clapping, when progress feels invisible, when pain seems louder than hope. Perseverance is saying, "I'll try again tomorrow," even after today broke you down.

That season became the foundation for how I live my life now. When storms come, and they always do, I don't panic the way I used to. I don't collapse under the weight of unfairness. Instead, I remind myself: You've been here before. You've faced the impossible, and you made it possible.

I use that perseverance as a mother. Parenting is its own marathon. I've had to keep showing up when my heart was exhausted, when my children's needs felt bigger than my resources, and when I wanted to protect them from storms I couldn't stop. I persevered through teenage rebellion, through nights when silence in the house was heavier than any argument, through the ache of watching them navigate pain I couldn't heal for them. Just like I did with my body, I had to stay present, step by step, even when it hurt. Perseverance taught me to parent not from a place of perfection, but from consistency and unconditional love.

I use perseverance in my career. I've walked into boardrooms where people underestimated me before I even spoke. I've led teams while carrying my own personal battles behind the scenes. I've juggled deadlines while raising children, balancing community work, and facing financial challenges that would have made some give up. But the same persistence that lifted my body off the bed when my spine was broken has carried me through every professional obstacle. I know how to keep moving when the odds say I shouldn't.

Perseverance has also shaped my leadership. It gave me the resilience to stand in spaces where my voice wasn't always welcomed. It gave me the courage to mentor others and to say, "I see you. I believe in you. And you are capable of more than you realize." Because perseverance doesn't just belong to me, it is something I now hand down to others.

I use it in relationships too. Love is not always smooth. Misunderstandings come, distance grows, and healing is required. Perseverance has taught me not to quit the first-time things feel heavy. It has taught me to communicate, to fight for clarity, and to choose forgiveness not because it is easy, but because it is worth it. Just like in my recovery, I've learned that progress in relationships comes in inches, not miles.

Most importantly, I use perseverance in how I show up for my community. My story has become my fuel. I mentor, I teach, I speak, I serve, all with the understanding that perseverance is contagious. People don't always need someone to hand them the answers. Sometimes they need someone who can look them in the eyes and say, "I've been through the fire too. You can survive this."

What I once thought was my greatest tragedy became my greatest training ground. Breaking my back could have broken my spirit, but instead it stretched it. It taught me that strength is not about being unshakable. It's about refusing to stay down when life knocks you flat.

Now, when storms rise in my life, I no longer fear them. I know storms don't just come to destroy. They come to reveal the strength that has been waiting inside me all along. My perseverance is no longer just a skill I use to get through the day. It is the rhythm of my life, the anchor that grounds me, the fire that lights my path.

And every time I face something new, I hear the same voice I heard when I stood shaking in that rehabilitation room: One step at a time. You already know how to survive this.

Latricia Ferris

What they called
broken was really
me being rebuilt

Beyond the Storm

Tsunami of Grief

"Some storms arrive with thunder in the sky, others with silence in the night. Either way, they leave the ground changed forever."

Affirmation: I honor every life I've lost by carrying their love forward, even through the pain.

The storm of gunfire was the first to show me how fragile life could be. At Auntie Redd's house, the air itself felt heavy, thick with cigarette smoke, fried food, and danger. Outside, sirens wailed like wolves. Inside, the grown-ups laughed too loudly, their eyes glassy, their hands twitching. The air was always unsettled, like a storm waiting to break.

One night, while I cradled my baby cousin on a sagging couch, the storm broke. A gunshot cracked through the living room window. Glass rained down, glittering like deadly snow. My body moved before my mind could catch up. I dropped to the floor, shielding the baby with everything I had. My heart pounded louder than the thunder outside.

Return fire erupted from the back room. My cousin, older and hardened by a world I barely understood, shoved a gun into my trembling hands. "If they come up the stairs and don't call your name," he said, voice sharp as lightning, "you shoot."

The weapon was heavier than anything I had ever held. Heavier than fear. Heavier than childhood. I pointed it at the door, hands shaking, breath trapped in my throat, whispering a prayer. Please, God, don't make me pull this trigger.

Minutes stretched like hours, but when my cousin finally called my name from the stairwell, I dropped the gun like it was made of fire. That night, I learned that storms don't just rage outside; they crash into your home, your innocence, and your soul. And that was only the beginning.

A few months later, another bullet storm found us. This time it came from our own family. One of my cousin's friends mistook my mom's car for a rival gangs because of the red Kansas City Chiefs jacket I was wearing. As we pulled into the driveway, shots rang out. Time slowed. I watched the car doors absorb the bullets like silent bodyguards. By some miracle, none of us was hit.

That was just the start of storms that would leave me carrying the weight of lives gone too soon.

The first death I ever witnessed was my great-grandmother's. I was fourteen, still unsure of myself, and she lay in hospice, her body frail but her eyes full of light. She told me she saw her parents and was going with them. Moments later, she took her last breath. It was peaceful, surreal. Death came as a quiet storm, and I didn't know then how often it would return.

When I was sixteen, death struck again. I walked into school and someone told me my friend Cathy had passed away. I tried to fight them because I thought they were lying. Just that Friday, we'd taken pictures together with our group of friends. Just that Sunday morning, we spoke. And then, Sunday night, her heart gave out. Cathy had this laugh that could light up a room. In the days after, I would sit in class pretending to listen, but all I heard was the echo of her laugh in my head. I handed in homework that didn't matter anymore. I smiled at people who couldn't feel the hollowness inside me. One of my best friends was gone, and I couldn't understand why.

Then came Fatso, my cousin but also my brother. We had spent the summer together, thick as thieves. He was more than family; he was my protector, my mirror, the one who always had my back. Shortly after returning to Texas, he was shot multiple times while sitting in a car. I still see him in my dreams, hear his voice in my memory. When I learned he was gone, I still had to get up the next day, fix breakfast, wash clothes, move through the motions of life, while inside I was empty. I folded laundry with tears running down my face, teaching myself how to keep living while dead inside.

And then Scooby, aka Verdell, my ex-husband's little sister's husband. Scooby was from Chicago, a natural hustler, a man who loved animals and filled his home with them. He was protective, caring, and always eager to learn. He had moved to Denver with us because his wife, CheQuita was pregnant, and they were building their life with their little ones. He loved family. He would do anything for family. And then violence took him too.

That night I was celebrating my birthday. Scooby had promised to meet us with a bottle of Hennessy XO. He was supposed to join us, but he got delayed. On his way, he decided to stop at his house before coming to see us. That was the last detour he ever made. I was driving home when

CheQuita called, her voice frantic, screaming, "He's been shot!" over and over. My heart dropped into my stomach, but I didn't know who she meant until she choked out his name. Scooby.

We sped down the road to University Hospital, my brother Steve and I were running inside, desperate for news. They were operating on him. I stayed with CheQuita night and day for weeks while he fought. The man who had been so full of life was now silent, tethered to machines. When he could finally whisper through his trach, he told us he had seen God, that he was going to pass, but that he would be alright. We didn't want to believe him. He said his goodbyes, and eventually, he slipped away. His children, too young to understand, visited him in the hospital, holding his hand while machines beeped around them. His youngest never got to know him. His oldest carries the grief in her eyes even now. His death hardened me. It made me fear for my kids at every party, every outing. It made me pray harder, because the world had shown me how quickly it could snatch life away.

Then cancer came for my grandmother, the rock of our family. She was small, 4'8" and 90 pounds, but she was the strongest person I knew. She was everything. I was her oldest grandchild, and my daughter was her first great-grandchild. My son was her first great-grandson. She spoiled them, poured love into them, and shaped them. She baked, sewed, and created with her hands. She couldn't read or write, but she made up stories that stuck with us forever. She taught us to give, even when we didn't have much ourselves. She would take us to the Goodwill on the first of the month when her SSI check came. Those were her ways of teaching generosity, joy, and resilience.

When she was first diagnosed with pancreatic cancer, they gave her six months. She lived ten more years. She said she wanted to take my son to the zoo for ice cream, and she did. For years after, every trip to the zoo meant a cone in her honor. But then came the lung cancer. Within five months, it claimed her life. I became her caregiver, moving in with her because we were both battling cancer together. My son's 10th birthday was celebrated in her home, her body weak on the couch, but her spirit alive, cheering him on. A week later, she asked me to send her to Denver Hospice. She said she would hold on for my daughter's birthday. She did. She died on November 7th, my daughter's birthday, her last gift to her.

Her death shattered us. Family rumors swirled that I had stolen from her, lies that tore us apart. Her sisters spread them, and for five years, most of my family stopped speaking to me and my kids. I buried her, paid for her funeral, and wrote her obituary. I carried her alone. Her absence left a hole in our holidays, in our everyday lives. For my kids, losing her was losing home itself. Even now, I see her birthday on clocks, in moments. She whispers strength to me. She whispers love.

And then came CJ. My nephew, my son's cousin, his best friend, his God brother. CJ was loving, funny, always in braids, riding motorcycles with his dad, playing football, laughing at every turn. He and Aron were the same age. They rode bikes together, joked endlessly, and loved dogs with the same passion. They were inseparable.

The night I got the call, I thought he had run away. My ex-husband's voice cracked when he said, "CJ is gone." I grabbed my keys, ready to search for him. Then the words hit: "No, Tricia, he's dead." My knees buckled. I collapsed onto the floor, sobbing so loud my daughter heard and came running. "What's wrong, Mom?" All I could say was his name. CJ. She froze in the hallway, her eyes wide with terror. My son was away at summer camp, three days from coming home. We decided to wait, to spare him until we could be there together.

When we picked him up, Aron climbed into the car, oblivious, glowing with the light of camp. "Mom," he said, "CJ came to play tricks on me. He kept turning out the lights. I can't wait to ask him how he did it when we get home." My heart split in two. Me and his dad broke. Tears rolled. Aron's face twisted with confusion. I climbed into the back seat, held his hands, and said the words no mother should have to say: "CJ passed."

He stopped breathing. His chest locked. His face turned pale. I shook him, begging, "Breathe, baby, breathe." He gasped finally, sobbing, collapsing into me. That moment will never leave me. The sound of his cry still rattles my bones. He cried and cried, and nothing I said could soothe him.

CJ's death became Aron's shadow. He poured his grief into music, writing songs in CJ's honor. His music went global, his pain immortalized. But grief still consumed him. He tattooed CJ's name on his body, alongside Pootie and Tre'Joun, the other cousins he would lose. Therapy helped, but never erased the hole. Some days, he didn't want to live. He leaned on Tre'Joun and Lazarus for strength, but CJ's absence never stopped aching.

My daughter grieved silently, swallowing her pain until it nearly killed her. A month later, she attempted suicide by pills. She spent a week in an inpatient facility. Then therapy, alone and as a family. I tried to hold us all together, but my hands were trembling, broken myself. CJ's death shook us to the core. It even made me and their dad reconcile briefly, canceling our divorce. We tried to rebuild, but grief was stronger than love. Within a year, we divorced anyway. For the family as a whole, CJ's death was the beginning of a long unraveling.

And then Tre'Joun. My light. My nephew, who was more like a son, who I taught to walk. Tre'Joun was funny, smart, and able to fix anything electronic. He loved Adventure Time, loved music, and loved his family. He treated his little brothers like his own children when they were born. He was a year younger than my daughter, her sparring partner, her sibling in everything but name. For Aron, he was a big brother, his music partner, and his role model. For me, he was my baby. He had a son of his own, and my daughter was his son's godmother.

The night he died, I was in a hospital with my cousin Nish, who was giving birth. My daughter called, crying, saying Tre had been shot and was at University Hospital. Police weren't letting the family in. Aron was with her. My stomach turned to ice. Then the doctor called me into the C-section room. Nish was delivering her son. I held it together for her, hiding my panic, knowing my daughter's next call would confirm the worst. When the baby was born, beautiful, albino, glowing, I smiled through my tears. My phone buzzed again. I knew. Tre was gone.

I exploded outside the room, collapsing on the floor in grief. Then I went to CheQuita's house, where everyone was gathered. My children were broken. My daughter spiraled, drinking heavily, clinging to Tre's friends for comfort. She blew up photos of him on canvas and hung them on her walls. She baked cakes in his honor, stepped up for his son,

122

and took her godmother role more seriously than ever. She tattooed his name on her skin. She cried for nights on end, hollow with loss.

Aron spiraled too. He was in college but dropped out, unable to focus. He popped pills, drank, numbed himself. His grief pulled him into darkness until he tried to take his own life. He crashed his car, called me, and was shaken but alive. When I saw him, I knew he was high, drowning. I called his dad, who took him to Colorado Springs to keep him safe. It wasn't until Aron wrote a song that I realized it had been a suicide attempt. His music became both his cry for help and his lifeline.

As a mother, I was torn in half. I was grieving my nephew, my child I had helped raise, while also trying to save my own children from drowning in grief. I held them, whispered to them, promised things I wasn't sure I could keep, that it would get better, that they were safe, that they'd survive this storm. But inside, I was as broken as they were.

All of these deaths, so many faces, so many storms, ripped through my life. My great-grandmother's peaceful passing, Cathy's sudden silence, Fatso's violent end, Scooby's stolen youth, my grandmother's legacy cut short, CJ's unbearable absence, Tre'Joun's stolen future. Each storm carried its own thunder, its own lightning, its own flood. Each reshaped me, my children, my family.

We tend to live like we have endless tomorrows. But I know differently. I've seen how fast laughter turns into silence. I've seen how quickly a heartbeat can become the last. These storms left me drenched in grief, carrying the weight of absence, carrying memories instead of people.

Grief is a storm that never truly passes. It shifts, it softens, but it doesn't disappear. I hold them all inside me, their smiles, their voices, their love. And though healing will come later, right now, I let the storm of grief stand as it is: heavy, unmovable, and real.

Category 5
Pause. Breathe. Reflect.

Grief has no clock. It sneaks into your mornings, your workdays, your quiet nights. It shows up in your children's questions, in an empty chair at the table, in the silence where a laugh used to be. It demands to be felt, yet so often we are forced to carry it quietly, smiling for others while bleeding inside.

This reflection is not about erasing grief. It's about letting yourself face it honestly. It's about naming the storms that shaped you, acknowledging the scars they left, and permitting yourself to heal.

Take your time with these questions. They may hurt. They may stir memories you've tried to bury. But if you allow yourself to sit with them, they can also open a door, not to forget, but to transform your pain into strength.

Journal Prompt

1: Who was the first person you lost, and what do you remember most vividly about that moment? (Did you feel shock, peace, confusion, or anger? Where were you when it happened? How did it change the way you looked at life?)

Journal Prompt

2: Think of someone you lost suddenly, without warning. What would you say to them if you had one more conversation? (Write them a letter. Let it be messy, loving, angry, grateful—whatever your heart needs to release.)

Journal Prompt

3: How did grief affect your day-to-day life? (Did you still have to go to work, take care of children, cook, or show up for others while you were breaking inside? Write about what it felt like to carry that invisible weight.)

Journal Prompt

4: How has loss shaped your family? (Were there moments where grief pulled you closer, or times where it created silence and distance? How did your children, siblings, or parents carry it? What did you carry for them?)

Journal Prompt

5: Think about the storms of grief that hurt the most. What coping mechanisms did you turn to? (Were they healthy, or did they numb the pain? Looking back, what do you wish you had permitted yourself to do?)

Journal Prompt

6: Imagine the person you lost standing with you right now. What would they want for your life moving forward? (Would they want you to stay stuck in grief, or to keep living with the love they left behind?)

Grief is not a storm you conquer. It is a storm you learn to carry, one you walk through again and again until the rain becomes less sharp, the thunder less deafening. By writing, remembering, and reflecting, you permit yourself to feel, and in feeling, you open the door to healing.

 **Latricia Ferris**

You can't bloom pretending it never rained

Beyond the Storm

After the Storm: Aftershocks of the Storm

"Grief does not vanish with time; it lingers like aftershocks, shaking us when we least expect it. But even in the trembling, we find our strength."

Affirmation: I honor my grief by turning it into love, my pain into power, and my storms into light.

The storm itself may pass, but the aftershocks remain. They ripple through the days that follow, some gentle tremors, others quakes that drop you to your knees. Grief is not one moment; it is a thousand moments. It's the numb mornings when I can't lift myself from bed, the tears that come without warning, the exhaustion that feels like a black hole in my chest. But it's also the laughter that slips out when I tell a story about CJ, the pride I feel watching Aron honor Tre'Joun through music, or the smile.

The Waves

Grief changed the way I walk through this world. On the bad days, it is heavy. It steals my breath, saps my energy, and makes me want to disappear under the covers. I feel a hollow ache so vast it seems endless, like a universe without stars. Sometimes I cry, sometimes I just lie still, numb. On those days, I let the storm have its way with me because fighting it only makes it worse.

But then there are the loving days. Days when I choose to lean into legacy instead of loss. I cook meals that taste like my grandmother's kitchen. I play the songs that CJ and Aron used to laugh to, their voices overlapping in my memory. I bake cakes with my daughter and see Tre'Joun's light in her smile. I remember Scooby's energy and choose to protect my family fiercely, like he did. These loving days remind me that their lives were more than their deaths. Their storms did not erase the sunshine they brought.

Spiritual Connection

Grief pushed me closer to Yahweh. I used to sit in church pews, but eventually I learned my connection with God was not confined to four walls. I found Him in the silence of meditation, in the pages of my journal, in the way my loved ones appeared in dreams. I heard them in the wind, felt them in numbers that repeated, 444, 1212, 1010, and 911, sacred signs that whispered, "We are still here."

I began collecting crystals, holding them in my palm when the nights grew long. I laid tarot cards not to predict the future but to hear my soul speak. I whispered affirmations into the mirror until I believed them. "You are strong. You are light. You are love." Each practice became a lifeline, a way to tether myself to the divine when the ground beneath me trembled. These practices reminded me that grief was not the end but a doorway to something deeper.

Bad Days vs Loving Days

I will not lie and say it is easy. The bad days are still bad. Some mornings I wake up and feel the weight of every loss pressing on my chest. I want to stay in bed, close the blinds, shut out the world. On those days, grief feels endless. I am tired. I am empty. The storm takes me back into its center, and I am powerless against its pull.

But then come the loving days, and they save me. I celebrate birthdays by lighting candles. I make my grandma's favorite meals, I smile at my son's tattoos that honor his cousins, I play Tre'Joun's music loud so the walls vibrate with his voice. I laugh at the way my CJ used to mispronounce words when he told his made-up stories. I let my children feel the love that lingers in those memories. These moments are proof that grief cannot erase love. Love always finds a way to shine through.

Turning Pain into Power

Grief taught me that time is our most valuable gift. None of us knows how much we have left. I once asked a class I was teaching at work, "If you never saw each other again, what memory would you want to leave behind?" That question is the compass I live by now. I want my memory in people's lives to be love, kindness, and support. I want them to say, "Latricia made me feel seen. She made me feel worthy."

So I pour into others. I've given furniture to strangers who had none. Bought groceries for families I didn't know. Given rides in the rain to elders who couldn't walk home. Some of these acts only me, the other person, and God know about. But they matter. They remind me that love is stronger than grief. This is the legacy I want to turn storms into shelter for others.

This philosophy bleeds into everything: my business, my community work, my family. It is why I am writing this book. I want others to lean on my strength when their storms come. I want them to know they are not alone, that survival is possible, and that storms can be transformed into power. Every scar I carry is now a lantern for someone else lost in the dark.

Family Growth

My children have carried grief beside me. Danajha pours love into her cakes, creating sweetness in a world that sometimes tastes bitter. Aron pours his heart into music, his songs becoming tributes that reach the world. They honor CJ, Tre'Joun, and others daily, not with silence but with creation. This is how grief reshaped us: we stopped burying love in the ground and started growing it into something new.

We talk often about death and legacy. We know that energy never dies, and neither does love. It was here before we were born and will be here after we take our last breath. We talk about free will and choice, about how we choose to live with love. This belief system carries us through. It keeps us from drowning when the waves come.

Legacy & Love

When I look back, I know what my loved ones would say: "We knew you would carry on with strength and love." I feel them encouraging me, reminding me that the world still needs the light I carry. I know their lives were not in vain because they live on through me, through my children, through the work I do every day.

When you see me, you see them. Their reflections are stitched into my very soul. Every kind word I give, every act of service I offer, every moment of strength I show, it is them. It is their legacy flowing through me. They are the roots that ground me, the wind that pushes me forward, the rainbow after every storm.

Aftershocks

The aftershocks of grief never end, but they no longer destroy me. Instead, they remind me of how deeply I have loved and been loved. Some days are heavy, others are light. Some days I crumble, others I soar. But every day, I carry them with me. And every day, I choose to turn pain into power.

The storm shaped me, but it did not break me. It made me stronger, softer, wiser. It made me a vessel for love. These aftershocks are not just reminders of what I lost, they are proof of what I have gained: resilience, compassion, and the unshakable belief that love is eternal.

"The storm will always leave its aftershocks, but I've learned that even trembling ground can grow new roots.

Healing is not about forgetting; it's about choosing love every day, even when grief whispers otherwise. And so, as I step out of the storm's shadow, I begin to walk toward the light that waits ahead."

I'm not who I was
before the storm,
and that's the
point

Beyond the Storm

134

Tornado Warnings

"Tornadoes are not random. They give warnings, sirens, and signs. The danger comes when we refuse to listen." – Unknown

Affirmation: I no longer ignore the sirens of my soul. When warnings come, I trust them and protect my peace.

The sky does not always darken before the storm. Sometimes it fools you with blue skies and still air, lulling you into thinking you are safe. Sometimes it looks gentle right before the winds rip through everything you thought was secure. Betrayal arrives in the same way, quiet, deceptive, almost soft, until suddenly, the air is different, the silence too sharp, and your world is torn apart.

I've learned that betrayal is it's own kind of tornado. Sudden. Violent. Relentless. It touches down in friendships you swore would last forever, in love you thought was safe, in workplaces where you poured loyalty and labor. And when it hits, it does not care about the years invested, the history written, or the love given. It tears through without hesitation, leaving debris where trust once stood.

What makes betrayal so devastating is not just the destruction. It's the warnings we chose to ignore. The uneasy silence. The change in the air. The gut feeling we dismiss as paranoia. We stay outside too long, convincing ourselves the sirens aren't meant for us, that maybe this storm will pass us by. And then the funnel drops, tearing through everything in its path, and by the time we finally run for cover, it's already too late.

This chapter is about those storms, the betrayals that shook my friendships, my work, and my love life. Each one left me standing in debris I never thought I'd face. But each one also taught me how to hear the sirens, how to trust them, and how to rebuild stronger than before.

The first betrayal came like a funnel cloud that everyone else could see but me. The sky had been shifting for years, with whispers of her turning on others, stories of sudden fallouts, and warning sirens blaring through the mouths of people who had known her longer than I had. I muted them all. I told myself those people must have deserved it. I told myself thirty years of friendship meant I was safe in the center of the storm. I thought loyalty was a shield strong enough to protect me. I was wrong.

I remember the day clearly. I had picked my son up from school, the afternoon light slanting across the pavement as he climbed into the car. We drove back to the house I rented from her, a place that felt secure, familiar, mine. I unlocked the door, dropped off a few things, and locked it again before heading back out. Nothing seemed unusual. Nothing warned me that within a few hours, the ground beneath me would shift.

When I returned later, the key I had always used scraped uselessly against the lock. It stuck, screeched, refused to turn. My heart pounded as I tried again, harder this time, my hand trembling with each attempt. The sound of metal grinding against metal was sharp and cold, like a siren blaring in my ears. My son stood beside me, confused, asking what was wrong. I pressed my palm against the door as if I could will it open, but it would not budge.

Through the narrow window, I caught a glimpse inside, and my breath caught in my throat. Dust floated in the air like smoke after a fire. The bathrooms had been gutted, the walls torn apart, the pipes hanging exposed like broken veins. The smell of plaster and wet wood drifted through the cracks, harsh and bitter. My home, the place I paid for and cared for, had been demolished without a word.

I felt my knees weaken under the weight of betrayal. This was not just a renovation. This was a deliberate act, carried out by the woman I trusted like family. My chest tightened with panic as I realized I had been locked out of my own home. I had to call the police just to get back inside. Even standing in front of the officers, explaining what had happened, I felt numb, as if the ground itself had split open beneath me.

For thirty years, she had been more than a friend. She had been a sister, a constant presence through birthdays, secrets, and tears. And now, in a single afternoon, that bond was reduced to rubble. Torn apart like the walls inside, ripped open by a storm I had convinced myself would never touch me.

The sirens had been there all along, but I chose not to hear them. Now I stood in the wreckage, realizing too late that loyalty could not stop destruction, and love could not keep the locks from changing.

Her words still echoed in my mind long after the call ended. It wasn't just the broken computer; it was the way she had tried to fracture the bond between me and my son with a single lie. That betrayal settled into me like heavy rain that refuses to stop, seeping into every corner of my spirit. I kept asking myself how many sirens I had ignored, how many red flags I had silenced in the name of loyalty.

And just when I thought I had learned enough about betrayal, another storm gathered, this time in my own bed.

Romantic betrayal cuts differently than friendship. It is quieter, more insidious. It doesn't always come with locks changed or glass shattered. Sometimes it comes with silence. The space between two people that was once filled with laughter, warmth, and whispers now feels like the air before a tornado, heavy and unnatural. You sense the shift, but you tell yourself it's nothing. You tell yourself the storm will pass.

I remember lying beside him, the hum of the television filling the space where conversation used to live. His body was near mine, but it felt miles away. His eyes wandered elsewhere, his phone lighting up with messages he suddenly had to hide. My spirit stirred with warnings, visions so clear they might as well have been written across the walls. I saw what was coming, but I convinced myself I was imagining it.

I told myself I was just paranoid. I told myself love meant trust, even when my chest ached with unease. The sirens inside me grew louder, but I turned up the volume of excuses, drowning out my own intuition. I stayed outside too long, ignoring the sky that was turning darker by the minute.

And then the funnel dropped.

The truth came crashing down, not in one explosive moment, but in fragments—missed calls, unexplained absences, the dull ache of realizing the intimacy we once shared had been replaced by cold silence. I was lying next to someone who had already left me in spirit, someone whose promises of forever scattered like debris in the wind.

That kind of betrayal doesn't just hurt. It hollows. It makes you question yourself, your worth, and your ability to trust again. I remember lying awake, staring at the ceiling, the silence around me louder than any storm outside. The love I had once believed in felt like it had been ripped away piece by piece, leaving me standing in wreckage I never saw coming, even though the signs had been there all along.

Betrayal in love feels like being lifted into the air by tornado winds, the ground gone, the world spinning, no safe place to land. And when you finally do, the silence after is deafening.

Romantic betrayal left me gasping for air, but storms don't only strike inside homes or hearts. They strike under fluorescent lights, too, in offices where you expect fairness and respect.

I remember sitting in that HR room, the air stale with the bitter smell of old coffee. The walls were bare, the lighting harsh, humming overhead like a low warning tone. My palms were damp against the table as I tried to steady my voice, forcing myself to speak up about words that had cut me to my core.

It wasn't just any insult. It was a racist comment, sharp and demeaning, meant to remind me of my place in a system that never wanted me to rise too high. It was a strike against my identity, against the very skin I live in every day. That kind of wound doesn't just sting; it carves deep, leaving scars that resurface long after the moment has passed.

I had gone in expecting justice. I had gone in believing the system would work, that the people in charge would hear me and act. Instead, I watched their eyes shift, cold and dismissive, as if my pain was an inconvenience. Their responses were clipped, detached, as though I were the problem for daring to bring it forward at all.

And then came the blow I did not expect. Instead of support, I was punished. Instead of fairness, I was silenced. They stripped away my position, tarnished my name, and spread lies about me as though my dignity were debris to scatter across the office floor.

Walking out of that building felt like stepping into gale-force winds, each gust tearing away another piece of hope I had held onto. I had clung so tightly to the belief that loyalty and hard work would be enough. But loyalty does not shield you from betrayal, and hard work does not stop storms from touching down.

Each day after was a battle against the winds. I showed up with a smile I did not feel, walked through halls heavy with whispers, and carried the weight of injustice in my chest. It felt like standing outside as the sky darkened, waiting for the funnel cloud to descend again, bracing myself for impact.

Eventually, I realized I could not survive standing in that storm. My grip on hope was leaving rope burns on my hands, but I held on until the pain became unbearable. And when I finally let go, I discovered something unexpected. I did not fall into destruction. I fell into freedom.

Sometimes survival is not about standing strong against the storm. Sometimes, survival is walking away before the walls collapse.

All of these tornadoes did not arrive one after another, giving me time to catch my breath. They came all at once, touching down across every corner of my life. While friendships collapsed and workplaces turned against me, I was also fighting for my health, dragging an oxygen tank as if it were an anchor chained to my body. In that same season, I buried four family members, grief piling on grief until my spirit felt buried under rubble. And in the middle of it all, one of my children was fighting his own mental battles, slipping into darkness while I tried desperately to keep him in the light.

I remember shutting down, not just emotionally but physically. The smallest things, combing my hair, stepping into the shower, even brushing my teeth, felt like mountains that required strength I did not have. Every step was heavy. Every day was survival. There was no sanctuary. Nowhere to exhale. It felt as if the storms were circling me, funnel after funnel dropping without mercy.

And yet, even in the chaos, I had to keep going. I had to hold myself together for my kids, even when I was unraveling inside. I carried grief in one hand and betrayal in the other, while trying to hide my trembling so they would not see how broken I was. Sometimes the weight was so heavy that one more small thing, an offhand comment, a bill arriving in the mail, a knock at the door, was enough to bring me to my knees.

That is what people don't always understand. We are not always fighting one battle at a time. Sometimes we are at war on every front, with our bodies, our families, our friendships, our jobs, and our own minds. And when that weight becomes unbearable, it is not weakness to break. It is human.

Betrayal feels like drowning, like being lifted by tornado winds with no ground to stand on. It feels like silence after the funnel lifts, standing in the wreckage of what used to be your life. But healing is possible. It comes slowly, like bricks laid one by one, rebuilding walls around a heart that learned the hard way.

For me, healing looked like learning to sit with myself and be okay. It looked like grieving the people I lost but honoring the woman I became in their absence. It looked like finally hearing the sirens in my spirit and choosing shelter instead of denial.

Tornado warnings are not meant to terrify us. They are meant to save us. And now, I no longer silence them. I honor them. I act on them. Because storms will come again, that is life. But destruction is not inevitable.

I am no longer the woman who waits outside, convincing herself the sky will clear. I am the woman who listens. Who trusts. Who moves when the sirens sound?

I am the woman who survives and rebuilds, carrying my children, my scars, and my spirit forward, stronger than before.

After the Twister
Pause. Breathe. Reflect.

Betrayals are storms that leave us standing in debris we never expected to face. They come in friendships, in love, in workplaces, and sometimes in our own families. And often, they come when other storms are already raging, piling weight on top of weight until even the smallest thing feels unbearable.

If you are here, if you are reading this, you have survived storms too. Maybe you silenced the sirens in your spirit. Maybe you ignored the warning signs because you loved too deeply, trusted too much, or believed that loyalty could protect you. We all have. But every storm leaves us with a choice—to stay broken in the wreckage or to listen differently next time.

Journal Prompt 1: Think of a time you ignored your inner warning signs. What did the "sirens" feel like in your body or spirit? What happened when you stayed too long?

Journal Prompt 2: Who in your life showed you their true colors, and you chose to see only their potential? What did that storm teach you about trust?

Journal Prompt 3: Where in your life are you still waiting outside in dangerous weather, hoping the sky will clear? What would it mean to move to safety now?

Journal Prompt 4: Betrayals often leave us questioning our worth. Write down three truths about who you are that no storm can take away from you.

Tools for Processing Betrayal

- **Body Check-In:** Notice where betrayal still lives in your body. Tight shoulders? Anxious stomach? Journal about it and release it with deep breathing.

- **Boundary Setting:** Write one "No" you need to say this week. Practice it out loud. Let it be a full sentence, standing on its own.

- **Reframe Loyalty:** Loyalty is powerful, but it should never come at the cost of your peace. Make a list of people who have shown loyalty *to you*, not just taken it from you.

- **Anchor Practice:** When storms of betrayal replay in your mind, anchor yourself with something steady—a verse, an affirmation, a grounding breath—to remind yourself the storm has already passed.

Closing Affirmation:

I no longer silence the sirens in my soul. I move when the warnings come. I protect my peace, and in doing so, I protect my future.

Latricia Ferris

Faith didn't remove my storm; it gave me shelter inside it

Beyond the Storm

147

After the Storm: Somewhere Over the Rainbow

"The sky always clears. The storm may break us, bend us, shake us, but it cannot last forever. The sun will rise, and with it, so will we." – Unknown

Affirmation: I am living proof that storms do not destroy me. They refine me. They strengthen me. They prepare me to guide others into the light.

The tornadoes left wreckage behind, but they did not leave me ruined. At the time, I could not see it. I remember the days when silence felt like quicksand, pulling me deeper with every breath. I remember staring at walls that seemed to close in, rooms that once felt safe now echoing with memories of betrayal and grief. My body was heavy, my spirit weary. Something as simple as combing my hair or stepping into a shower felt like climbing a mountain with no summit in sight.

I whispered prayers at night, not because I felt strong, but because I was desperate. Some days, I was convinced I had already lost the fight. Hopelessness sat on my chest like a weight I could not lift. Back then, I thought storms

148

destroyed you completely, and all you could do was crawl through the wreckage and hope to survive.

But I was wrong.

What I did not realize then was that storms do not just take. They are also clear. They tear down walls that were never steady. They strip away what was never rooted in love. They break apart foundations built on lies and force you to build again, this time on truth.

The people I lost, the ones I once called friends, were not truly friends at all. When the winds took them, it hurt, but I see now that space had to be made for something better. In their place came people who loved me openly and poured into me as much as I poured into them. Friends who check on me, who celebrate my wins, who show up without keeping score. Reciprocal love. Energy that matches mine.

The house I once lost was replaced by a home that felt like a promise fulfilled. I remember walking through the front door of that modern space for the first time. Clean lines. Open rooms filled with light. Stainless steel appliances gleaming. Hardwood floors smooth beneath my feet. A place with every detail I had dreamed of but never thought I would receive. It was more than shelter. It was a reminder that I had survived and that beauty was still possible on the other side of destruction.

The job that broke me with lies and racism was replaced with a role that honored my work and my worth. I can still recall the moment I saw my first paycheck with the raise that came with it. I sat in my car, staring at the numbers, tears streaming down my face. Not just because of the money, but because it was proof. Proof that I was valuable. Proof that I had not been diminished by what was done to me. Proof that the storm could strip me of a position but not of my purpose.

Even love was transformed. Once I released what was not real, I learned to love myself so deeply that I could no longer accept anything less from a partner. I stopped begging for scraps of affection and instead demanded the feast of genuine love. I stood taller. I walked away faster. I smiled at my own reflection and whispered, "You are enough," until I believed it with every fiber of my being.

It is like holding a cup filled with dirty water. For years, I kept trying to add clean water, believing it would eventually wash away the filth. But no matter how much I poured in, the water stayed murky, contaminated by what I refused to release. The truth was simple: the cup had to be emptied, scrubbed clean, and made ready to hold something new. Once I dumped out the dirt, once I scrubbed away the residue of betrayal, grief, and self-doubt, my blessings flowed in. They had been waiting all along for me to clean my cup.

And now I live with a cup that overflows.

One day not long ago, I sat across from a woman who was drowning in her own storm. Her shoulders sagged under invisible weight. Her eyes were tired, hollow in the way only grief and betrayal can carve. She spoke of hopelessness, of feeling like everything around her was collapsing. And as she spoke, I saw myself in her. I remembered the heaviness of dragging myself through each day. I remembered wondering if the storm would ever pass.

But this time, I was not the one drowning. I was the one holding the lantern.

I leaned in and shared with her the tools I had picked up in the wreckage. Breathing exercises to calm the panic. Affirmations to rebuild confidence. Boundaries to guard her peace. Resources to remind her she was not alone. As I spoke, I watched her eyes shift. I saw something flicker to life. It was not joy, not yet. But it was a belief. Belief that she, too, could make it through.

That is what the storm gave me. Not just scars. Not just stories. It gave me the ability to guide others, to say with confidence, "I have been there, and you will survive too."

Looking back now, I can see the strength that hopelessness once blinded me to. I see a woman who faced betrayal in every form, buried loved ones, battled her body, and still stood tall for her children. I see someone who should have crumbled under the weight of it all but chose instead to rise.

Clear skies do not mean storms will never return. They will. But I no longer fear them. My life elevated when I released what was not for me. I carry proof that no storm lasts forever, and when the winds are quiet, I will still be standing. Stronger. Wiser. Elevated. Unshakable.

And here is the truth I carry now. Blessings cannot pour into a life that is already overflowing with what drains you. To allow them in, you must first empty your cup. Release the friendships that only take. Release the jobs that diminish your worth. Release the relationships that silence your soul.

It will feel like a loss at first, but it is clearing. It is making space. The blessings waiting for you cannot arrive until you create room for them to land.

So open your hands. Dump out the dirty water. Clean your cup. And then, stand ready. Because when you do, the blessings will not trickle in. They will pour.

Latricia Ferris

Every ending carried me closer to the version of me I prayed for

Beyond the Storm

153

Earthquakes of Motherhood

"An earthquake does not ask permission before it shakes your world. "

Affirmation: Even when the ground crumbled beneath me, I held on to my children and we rose again.

The night was ordinary until it wasn't.

The streets in Saddle Rock Ridge always felt uneasy to me. Too new, too quiet, as if the ground hadn't settled yet under all that fresh concrete. Rows of cookie-cutter houses with identical faces, street names that twisted into each other like a cruel joke, Sicly Court, Sicly Road, Sicly Street. Each one was a copy of the last. Even with porch lights flickering on, the neighborhood was dimly lit, shadows swallowing the curbs and driveways. I still remember the way the wind felt that evening, a little too cool for the season, brushing my skin as if whispering a warning I couldn't understand at the time.

Inside, I tried to carry the weight of a house that was too big for one woman with a broken back and two children. My husband was locked away, my body still healing, and though I had stretched myself to fill the space, the truth was I was crumbling in places no one could see. The house echoed with emptiness. Even though toys were scattered in corners and my children's laughter sometimes filled the rooms, there was an undeniable hollowness that pressed against me. The air smelled faintly of laundry detergent and candles I kept burning to chase away the heaviness.

When "Uncle K" offered to help, I let him in. I knew his history, stolen cars, reckless choices, but I had never known him to cross the line with me. He was family, or at least that's what I had always told myself. In our world, titles like "uncle" weren't always about blood; they were about survival, about who showed up and who didn't. I clung to that small comfort, the way a person might cling to the frame of a doorway when the ground trembles.

That night, my family from Texas couldn't find my home. Their headlights cut through the maze of wrong turns until they gave up and called from a McDonald's nearby. I told my son to come ride with me. He was only five, a mama's boy who usually never wanted to leave my side, but this time he whined and clung to his video game controller like it was glued to his palms. His tears made me pause, but Uncle K spoke smoothly, saying, "Let him stay. You'll only be twenty minutes." His voice was casual, steady, too steady. I remember thinking how reassuring it sounded, how easily I let those words settle over my doubts.

It seemed harmless. Twenty minutes. Just long enough to grab fries, hug my cousin, and lead her through the winding streets back to my house.

The Durango's engine growled as I pulled away from the curb, leaving my son standing small and stubborn in the glow of the TV screen. I had no idea I was leaving the earth beneath us split wide open.

When I returned, the house was still. Too still. Silence in a home where children live is never just silence; it is absence. I set the McDonald's bags on the kitchen table, grease seeping into the paper, the scent of fries hanging heavy in the air. That smell would haunt me later, forever tied to this night. I called out for my son. No answer. I called for my uncle. Silence.

My cousin's voice carried from the living room: "Girl, this house is nice." But her words floated over me like static. I opened the back patio door and stepped into the cool night air, peering into the dark backyard. The grass whispered under the wind, but no sound of my son's laughter, no footsteps, no life.

Panic started as a tremor in my chest. Maybe they were upstairs. I ran through every room, loft, bedroom, closet, and yanking doors open, my breath coming short and sharp. My voice cracked as I shouted his name, but the house only echoed it back to me. The creak of doors, the thud of my feet on the carpeted stairs, the rushing of blood in my ears, it all became part of the earthquake building inside me.

By the time I reached the garage, the tremor inside me had become a full quake. My 4-door car was gone.

For a moment, a false calm settled in, like the eye of a storm. Maybe they just went to the store. I dialed my uncle's number. It rang into nothing. Again, and again. No answer. Minutes dragged their nails across the clock. My cousin watched me pace, her calm face a cruel contrast to the terror clawing up my throat.

The food on the table went untouched. The fries grew cold. My body folded into the couch but couldn't rest, every muscle tense, my ears straining for sounds that would never come. Calls to family yielded the same hollow response: "No, haven't seen them."

When the second hour passed, I broke. I called the police.

The house filled with officers asking questions that scraped me raw. What was he wearing? Do you have a picture? What color is your car? Each answer felt like another crack opening under me, my foundation giving way. My son was five. Five. How could he just vanish?

They told me to stay put in case he was returned. So, I sat. From 8 p.m. to nearly noon the next day, I sat frozen on that couch, eyes swollen from crying until they burned, rocking and praying. The room reeked of cold McDonald's grease, but I couldn't eat. I could only whisper bargains to God in between sobs: Bring my baby back. Take me instead. Just let me hold him again.

Time bent. Seconds bled into minutes, minutes into hours, until the officer's radio crackled like a fault line splitting open: They found the car.

Downtown. Across from the bus station. A place crawling with crime. They couldn't see inside because of the limo tint. No response when they knocked on the glass.

I broke apart. My breath came jagged, shallow, as if the quake had sucked the air out of the room. My father was nearby, he said. He would go.

I clutched the phone as he walked toward the car. I imagined the worst: an empty seat, a shadow of my son, a silence too heavy to bear. And then.

"Papa!" My son's voice, alive, bursting through the line when my father opened the door. Relief crashed through me, a tidal wave after hours of shaking earth. My legs gave out. My sobs tore from the deepest part of me. He was alive. Alive.

When they brought him home, he smelled of urine. The officers tried to speak gently, but his small voice shook: "I didn't open the door because I didn't want to get kidnapped again."

My heart cracked all over again.

And then he looked at me. "I'm mad at you."

The words pierced like glass under my skin. I thought he blamed me for leaving him, for trusting the wrong person. My apology rushed out, tangled and desperate. But he shook his head. "I'm not mad about that. I'm mad you hurt your eyes."

He had seen my swollen, bloodshot face, and in that moment, his small hands reached for the ice dispenser, filling his little hand with ice to press against me. Even in his fear, he thought of me. That memory still shakes me more than the quake itself.

He crawled into my lap, the ice melting between his fingers and mine, water dripping onto our clothes. I could feel his little body trembling against me, his heartbeat a wild drum against my chest. I wrapped my arms around him and rocked, back and forth, back and forth, like I used to when he was a baby and colic kept him awake at night. For a few minutes, we didn't speak. The officers moved quietly around us, their radios hissing, but the world narrowed to just me and him, breathing in sync.

Outside, daylight had finally broken. Through the blinds, the sun painted stripes of gold across the carpet, turning the living room into a place I barely recognized. The same walls that had felt like a prison the night before now held a strange kind of sanctuary. I could smell the cold grease of the forgotten food on the table, the faint metallic tang of the officer's badges, but under it all was the familiar scent of my son's hair pressed against my cheek.

"You're safe now," I whispered into the crown of his head, over and over until the words stopped shaking. "Mama's got you. You're safe." My tears slid down onto his face, and he wiped them away with his little thumb the way I'd once wiped his. His small act of comfort cracked something inside me open; in that moment, I wasn't just his protector, he was mine too.

When the officers finally asked their last questions and stepped out, we stayed there a long time. The house was still dim, but the tremor in my chest began to ease. My father came and sat across from us, his eyes wet but steady. Family began to arrive, bringing blankets, water, and soft words. No one could undo what had happened, but their presence was an anchor in the aftershock.

Later that day, after the paperwork and the statements, after my son had bathed and changed, he climbed onto my bed and fell asleep mid-sentence, his little fist still curled around the toy the officers had bought him. I watched him sleep, chest rising and falling, and in that quiet, I promised myself two things: I would never let fear be the language of our home, and I would teach him that even after the ground splits, you can rebuild.

That night changed everything. Trust became harder. The world seemed sharper, louder. But it also planted a seed of resilience I didn't know we had. We went to therapy. We learned new ways to breathe through panic, to name our fears instead of letting them grow silent and dark. Slowly, we began to live again, not as victims, but as survivors.

My uncle did a few years in jail and eventually got out. Still to this day, it hurts to hear his name. After a while, most of my family went back to dealing with him as if nothing ever happened. It hurts, if I'm being honest, but I know it didn't happen directly to them. Maybe that's why it's easier for them to look away. For me, though, it's a wound that time can't quite close. It's a reminder that sometimes family doesn't return to what it once was. Some fractures remain, even after the shaking stops. Some parts of us stay divided, not out of anger, but out of truth.

When the Ground Trembles
Pause. Breathe. Reflect.

There are moments in life that shake us so hard the ground beneath us never feels steady again. The night my son was taken was one of those moments. For months after, every phone call, every late text, every time he played outside for too long, my breath caught like the air itself could turn on me. Fear built its own house inside my chest.

Motherhood is its own kind of earthquake. It cracks open parts of you that you didn't know could break and somehow teaches you to rebuild stronger than before. After my son was found, the world didn't instantly go back to normal. I was still trembling inside. The sound of tires rolling on gravel could take me back to that night. The smell of fast food could bring tears to my eyes. The body remembers trauma even when the mind tries to move on.

But healing, real healing, is possible. It doesn't mean forgetting or pretending the quake never happened. It means learning how to live again without waiting for the next shake.

♡ Healing Tools

1. **Therapy and Honest Conversation**
   Sitting in therapy was the first time I let someone outside my circle see how deep the cracks ran. My son and I learned that healing isn't about erasing pain—it's about

161

giving it language. Therapy gave us that. It gave him a place to name his fear and permitted me to stop being the strong one all the time. For anyone carrying their own earthquake, therapy is not a weakness. It is rebuilding. It's the steady hands that help you re-stack the pieces when you're too tired to lift them alone.

2. Faith and Release

Prayer became my grounding. On nights when sleep wouldn't come, I whispered, "Thank You for bringing him home." Gratitude became my anchor. I couldn't change the past, but I could honor the miracle of survival. Releasing the "what ifs" and "why me" doesn't happen overnight, but over time, faith quiets the noise of guilt and replaces it with peace.

3. Community Support

Healing often hides in the presence of people who show up. I learned to let my village hold me. Friends who brought food, family who checked in, officers who cared about my son's safety—they became my temporary foundation while I built my own again. If you're walking through your own storm, let people in. It's not a weakness to accept help; it's wisdom.

4. Grounding Techniques for Overwhelming Moments

When anxiety returned, and it often did. I practiced grounding. These techniques brought me back to the present when my mind drifted to the "what ifs."

- **The 5-4-3-2-1 Method:**
  - Name *five* things you can see.
  - *Four* things you can touch.
  - *Three* things you can hear.
  - *Two* things you can smell.
  - *One* thing you can taste.
    It sounds simple, but it trains your brain to come back to now.

- **Box Breathing:**
  - Inhale for 4 counts, hold for 4, exhale for 4, hold again for 4.
  - Repeat until your heart slows down. Breathing retrains the body to know you are safe in this moment.

- **Safe Word or Touchstone:**
  I kept a small crystal in my pocket, a reminder of stability. For you, it might be a ring, a pendant, or a

smooth stone. Something to hold when the memories shake loose again.

5. Reclaiming Joy Through Routine
Once fear steals your peace, it tries to take your joy too. I fought back by rebuilding the structure. Morning sunlight, breakfast together, bedtime stories, and small laughter. Joy is not denial—it's resistance. It's proof that the quake didn't destroy everything.

🕊 Rebuilding the Foundation

Trauma cracks the foundation of trust—not only in others but in ourselves. After the kidnapping, I doubted every decision. I replayed that night over and over. Healing meant forgiving myself. I had to remind myself that I didn't cause this. Someone else's choices were their own demons, not mine to carry.

I learned that strength isn't about never falling apart. It's about letting the pieces settle and choosing to rebuild, even if your hands are still shaking.

Over time, therapy helped me understand how trauma hides in everyday life. My son and I learned to talk about fear without letting it define us. He grew stronger, and so did I. The love between a mother and child can rebuild anything—even after the ground splits open.

Journal Prompt 1:

When was the last time your world shook beneath you? What did that moment teach you about yourself, your faith, or your strength?

Journal Prompt 2:

Write a letter to the version of you who lived through that earthquake. What would you say to her now that she's on the other side?

Journal Prompt 3:

What does safety look and feel like for you today? How can you create that feeling intentionally?

Journal Prompt 4:

List five grounding practices that bring you peace when anxiety rises. Which one can you commit to using this week?

Journal Prompt 5:

What does forgiveness mean to you, not for others, but for yourself?

Closing Thought

When the earth breaks, it doesn't mean you are broken beyond repair. It means you have felt something powerful enough to change your landscape. The cracks may stay visible, but so will the flowers that grow through them.

You and your children are proof that even after the worst tremors, life can still bloom. Healing is not forgetting the earthquake. It's learning to dance again on the ground that remains.

66 **Latricia Ferris**

You can't be the storm and the calm, choose which one heals you

Beyond the Storm **99**

After the Storm: The Rebuilding Season

"What once broke the ground beneath us became the soil where our roots grew stronger. "

Affirmation: The storm tried to bury us, but we were seeds. We rose higher, brighter, and braver than before.

The morning sunlight poured into the kitchen, golden and warm, stretching across the countertop like it was blessing everything it touched. I could hear the faint sound of music playing from Aron's room, something soulful with a steady rhythm. That rhythm reminded me of peace. The air smelled of coffee and cinnamon, and for the first time in a long time, I realized I wasn't rushing anywhere. There was no crisis to fix, no chaos to manage, just a quiet morning filled with the sound of life moving forward.

The storm had passed, and this was what rebuilding felt like. It wasn't loud or grand. It was the softness of laughter echoing through a once-broken home, the stillness of morning light finding new ways to shine through the cracks. The quake that had once shaken our world no longer defined us. We had rebuilt on stronger ground.

Aron was six when the world began to show me what survival could look like in motion. His teachers had pulled me aside, their smiles wide and voices full of excitement, telling me that my baby was testing well beyond his grade level. They talked about his mind the way people describe something rare, precious, like a gift you only see once in a generation. He was reading novels meant for older kids, solving math problems that made my head spin, and asking questions that made even adults pause before answering.

But more than his intelligence, it was his heart that amazed me. He cared deeply. He loved gently. He carried the memory of that night, the fear, the silence, but he never let it define him. Instead, he used it as a quiet kind of strength. I knew he was special long before anyone said it out loud. But hearing others see what I had always known filled me with something close to awe.

When they suggested moving him up to fifth grade, I smiled and nodded, but a part of me hesitated. He was brilliant, yes, but he was still my little boy. I wanted him to be challenged, but I also wanted him to still have the chance to laugh, to play, to just be a kid. Childhood shouldn't have to rush. So, we found a balance, a school that saw his light and nurtured it without dimming his joy.

That's how we found Porter Billups Leadership Academy. He started there in fourth grade, and I still remember the first morning I dropped him off at Regis University for the summer program. He had his backpack slung over one shoulder, his hair freshly cut, his face full of curiosity. The campus was buzzing with kids, and for a moment, I just stood there watching him walk toward the school bus, sunlight catching the back of his head. It hit me then, he was stepping into a world that once felt impossible for us to reach.

Every summer, he returned to that same campus, surrounded by mentors who believed in him. Porter Billups wasn't just a program; it was a foundation that built character and confidence. It was the first place that showed my son he could belong anywhere his dreams took him. Each summer, he grew taller, wiser, and surer of himself. He'd come home talking about leadership, goals, college, and purpose. He didn't just want to succeed; he wanted to lead.

When the day came that he earned a full-ride scholarship to college, it felt like the earth itself celebrated. I cried tears of joy that morning, different tears than the ones I had shed years before. These were tears of victory, of gratitude. God had turned pain into purpose right before my eyes.

In sixth grade, Aron earned another scholarship, this time to attend Colorado Academy, one of the most prestigious private schools in Denver. I was nervous. It was a new environment, a new world filled with wealth and privilege. I didn't know if he'd fit in, if he'd be accepted, but my son didn't walk in with fear. He walked in with grace and confidence. From the first day, he carried himself like he belonged there, because deep down, he knew he did.

The years at Colorado Academy molded him into a leader. He found new challenges and learned how to navigate spaces that weren't always built for kids like him. In eighth grade, when he told me he was learning French, I smiled and teased, "Parlez-vous français?" He grinned, replying with words I didn't understand, and I tried to guess the meaning. Months later, he told me about a school trip to Quebec, Canada. My baby, my little boy who once wouldn't open a door for a stranger, was now boarding a plane to explore another country and culture.

When he returned, he couldn't stop talking about it: the cold air, the food, the way people switched between languages mid-sentence. He told me about standing in the streets of Quebec, feeling the world open up around him. "Mama," he said, "I felt free." And I remember thinking, that's all I ever wanted for you.

In his senior year in high school, through Porter Billups, he met Grammy Award-winning producer Bryan Kennedy. Even now, I can still see the excitement on his face when he told me he had been invited to California to record music. I watched him pack his suitcase, headphones, notebook, and dreams, and I traveled with him to California. Pride swelled in my chest so deep it hurt. Watching him walk in front of me to board a plane and go on a trip, completely paid for due to his work, was amazing. I realized he was no longer the little boy I'd once held through trembling nights. He was a young man chasing purpose.

The first time I heard his voice through a speaker, singing words he had written, I cried. His music carried pieces of our story, hope, struggle, and faith. The melodies were smooth but powerful, a reflection of everything we had endured. That sound wasn't just a song. It was healing. It was freedom.

Years passed, and Aron's creativity only grew. He began producing music for other artists, creating sounds that reached beyond Colorado, beyond ocean borders. He started his own production company and later launched a photography and videography business. I watched him work behind the camera with focus and passion, capturing people in their best light, something poetic about that, given how long it took for us to find our own.

Sometimes, late at night, I'd scroll through his photos online. I'd see the smiles he captured, the movement, the raw beauty. His art reflected what I had always hoped to teach him: that light is strongest after the darkness. Every image, every beat of his music, felt like a declaration that we survived, and not just survived, we thrived.

At twenty, Aron had built a life that once existed only in my prayers. He was his own man, disciplined, kind, and determined. But beneath all his success, he never lost the tenderness that defined him. He still checks on me, still hugs me before leaving, and still says I love you when walking out the door. The world had expanded for him, but his heart stayed close to home.

There are nights when I sit on the couch, and he's in his studio, laughter spilling down the hallway. I close my eyes and listen. The sound of his voice, his joy, his peace, fills the house the way the silence once did. The same walls that once echoed with fear now vibrate with music, laughter, and life. We had rebuilt the home and, in many ways, rebuilt ourselves.

Through therapy and time, I learned to trust again. Not easily, not quickly, but honestly. Healing doesn't happen overnight. It's built one breath, one prayer, one moment of choosing peace over pain. Watching Aron thrive became part of my healing. He was living proof that storms can shake us, but they can't destroy what's rooted in love.

Over time, my family went back to dealing with my uncle as if nothing had ever happened. They saw him at gatherings, laughed with him, and shared meals. But I couldn't. It wasn't about hate; it was about truth. Some storms pass, but the fault lines remain. Family can fracture in ways that never fully mend. I've made peace with that. Not every bond is meant to be repaired.

I learned that forgiveness doesn't always mean reconciliation. Sometimes it means accepting that you can love people from a distance. It means setting boundaries that protect your peace. I don't carry hate, but I carry memory. And that memory reminds me of who I am now, a woman who survived what was meant to break her, a mother who turned her pain into power.

Now, when I look at Aron, I see more than success. I see legacy. I see hope carried forward. I see the miracle of resilience written in flesh and blood. I see a living reminder that even when the ground crumbles, love can rebuild it brick by brick.

The night is quiet again. The storms have calmed. I watch my son work under the soft glow of his studio lights, his face focused, his spirit free. And in that peace, my heart swells with gratitude. The same hands that once trembled in fear now create, build, and inspire. That is the beauty of the rebuilding season. That is grace in motion.

As I sit in that stillness, pride wrapped around me like a blanket, a flicker of memory stirs, a night from long ago, a pain I'd buried deep. I glance toward the window, where the moonlight stretches across the floor, and I feel it again, the echo of another storm waiting in the distance. My heart tightens, not from fear but from knowing. Another story is coming, one that will shake me in new ways. But for now, I breathe in the peace of this moment, the calm before the next eruption.

After the storm, I
didn't just survive,
I started to live
out loud

Beyond the Storm

Volcano Eruption

"Some eruptions cannot be stopped; they burn everything in their path before the ash settles."

Affirmation: Even when the fire tried to consume us, I stood in the flames with my daughter, and together we rose from the ashes.

The day the ground burned through the floorboards began like any other. It did not come with sirens or a trumpet of warning. It came with the quiet rituals of survival. I was home from the hospital, stitched and stapled where my womb had been, body aching from surgery, lungs fed by tubing, and belly bruised from blood thinner shots. A woman in recovery. A mother who still had to be a mother. When you are a mother, you get up even when you cannot. You bake chicken even when the heat makes your scars throb. You tell your children yes to a movie, and you pretend that the living room light is enough to keep the monsters away.

He had helped with the chicken. He laughed at the corny parts of the comedy. He hugged me before he said he was leaving. He knew my kids, and he knew our routines. He had been around. He had earned a small slice of trust. Enough to sit on a couch and pass a plate. Enough to carry a bag of groceries in. Enough to say I will check on your place while you are in the hospital and have the keys to prove it.

I went to bed around eleven with the heaviness of pain medication turning my limbs into stone. I told the kids they could finish the movie, but to keep the volume low. They nodded. I kissed the air between us and closed my door. The garden level unit held its night sounds like it always did. The refrigerator hummed. The baseboard heat ticked. The leather sectional in the living room sighed when someone shifted. I slept because my body had demanded it. I slept because I believed we were safe.

Sometime around one in the morning, I woke up to use the bathroom. I saw both of my kids still awake. I told them to turn off the television and go to bed. I remember my voice sounding soft and tired. I remember the shape of my daughter's face in the bluish glow from the TV. I remember my son's blanket pulled up under his chin. I did not know that one sentence would be the line in the ash where a life breaks into before and after.

When the police arrived, I did not know why. I heard a man calling the name of the man who had helped the night before, and I thought I was dreaming. My eyes adjusted to sunlight that was not there, and a voice said Denver Police. The air thinned. I sat up and saw him in my bed in a white shirt and basketball shorts. I had no memory of him coming back. I remembered only the keys in his pocket and the door that could be opened by the wrong hands.

I shoved his shoulder and said the police are here. A gun pointed down my hall looked like a dark tunnel that swallowed sound. They cuffed him in front of me. An officer took my arm and said Ma'am, we have to get you outside. This is a crime scene. I asked where my kids were, and panic rose on top of the oxygen feeding my breath. He said they were safe in two cars. My alarm chimed to remind me to take my medication and give myself my shot. I told the officer, and he stood by while I slid a needle into bruised skin with shaky hands. Then we walked outside, where cold morning air met the taste of metal on my tongue.

My son was in a squad car. My daughter was in another. A woman who looked like my sister sat with my daughter. The officer noticed the confusion on my face and said it was my sister. I stared because she lived across town. I asked what was going on. He said we will tell you shortly. For now, you need to come with us. They put me in the back seat with my son and told me not to talk to him except to say it will be okay. The city slid past the window. I held my breath without meaning to.

They took us to a house that looked like a home daycare. There were tiny chairs, a tiny round table, and a bookshelf with children's books. There was a camera in the corner. I stood there in pajamas and a bonnet, an oxygen tube against my cheeks, and tried not to shake. A tall woman with blonde hair and a calm voice walked in with a badge on her belt. She told me to sit, and I did because my legs had started to tremble.

She asked me to recount the night. I told her about the chicken, the comedy, the hug, the goodbye at nine, the bathroom at one, and telling my children to go to bed. I told her I woke up to police in my hallway and a man in my bed who should not have been there. She asked me if I knew a name. I did not. She showed me a picture of the man I had been dating. She asked what his name was. I gave her the name on his passport. The name I believed. Then she told me the truth. He had sexually assaulted my daughter.

The chair scraped the floor when I stood. I threw it against the wall because the fire that lived in my spine jumped straight to my hands. I shouted that they should have told me earlier. I shouted that they let him walk away. I wanted to burn the air that had ever carried his breath. She kept her distance and spoke gently. He is in jail. We did not let him walk away. Your daughter is in the other room giving a statement. We will take you both to the clinic for an exam.

Everything after that moved like a horror film. Sound narrowed to a ringing in my ears. My daughter ran from the other room and folded herself into me. She was shaking and crying. I felt her ribs under my hands. I told her I was sorry. I told her I was here. I told her we would hold on. We got into the squad car again and drove a few blocks to an old brick clinic that felt frozen in time. The walls smelled like bleach and paper. The nurse asked my daughter to change into a gown. They explained that they had to keep her undergarments. They would give her replacements after. My daughter looked at the instruments and the swabs and the metal stirrups, and I saw her childhood drift two inches farther away.

I held her hand while a woman doctor and a nurse swabbed the places that should have been off limits to the world. She tensed, then tried to breathe. I told her to look at my eyes. It was over in minutes, but the memory will last a lifetime. They gave her new clothes, and we returned to the house that looked like a daycare to gather my son and my sister. We drove back toward my home. It was quiet except for crying and sniffles. When we pulled up, an officer stopped us. The house was still being processed. We could not go inside. We turned and went to a relative's house a few blocks away.

In that living room, my daughter told me what happened. I called a chaplain to connect us with her father in prison because I did not want her to have to repeat her story over and over. I wanted him to hear it once, from both of us, during a call that would change our family forever. She sat upright, brave and trembling. She said that after I told them to go to bed, she had been on the phone with a friend. She heard the front door open and assumed it was him. He walked into my room and closed the door. She went to the bathroom and then back to her room. She told me that he called her once to turn off a light that was already off. She ignored it. He called again and told her to turn off the bathroom light. This time the light was on. She was confused because she knew she had turned it off. She went to the bathroom. The door was slightly open. When she reached a hand in to flip the switch, he pulled her inside.

He told her to be quiet. He asked if she had ever been with a man. She was twelve. She shook her head no. He pulled down her pants and touched places that were not his to touch. He pulled them back up and told her to be quiet. He led her to the living room ottoman and touched her again. She cried. He told her to pull her pants back up. He told her to go to her room and to keep quiet. He told her he would buy her anything if she kept the secret. She nodded, went to her room, and closed the door.

When my children were little, I taught them what to do if someone ever tried to hurt them. I said go along with what they say until you are safe. Then tell. She did exactly that. She called my sister and another aunt. She called the police. She told them I was asleep and had no idea. She was protecting me while protecting herself, a child carrying the weight of a crime she never asked for.

After we ended the call with her father, I asked her why she did not scream. She said, "Because you would have killed him, and then I would have two parents in jail." She was right. There is a version of that night where I wake up and become a headline. I do not know how to write the word mercy over that possibility. I only know that my daughter saved both of us from a future we did not deserve.

180

The courts moved like slow lava. I showed up to every hearing because I had vowed to stand in the fire with my child. At first, there was talk of a deal. I did not want a deal. I wanted justice. He had used a false name. He had a passport that was not real. He had a past that looked different once the lie peeled back. In the end, the judge gave him the maximum. Ninety-six years. The charge was sexual assault on a minor by a person in a position of trust. The sentence felt both heavy and not heavy enough. Time cannot return what was taken. Time can only mark the distance from the moment the Earth split.

In the weeks after the assault, my daughter hovered near me. She slept with a light on. She did not want to be out of my sight. She could not find words for the pain. Her innocence felt stolen in a way that made ordinary objects change shape. The bathroom door was no longer a door. The ottoman was no longer a place to rest feet. The hallway was no longer a hallway. It was a fault line.

I watched her try to fold back into childhood and fail because the seams would not hold. I held her and scheduled therapy. I called anyone who could help. I prayed with a voice that was hoarse and low. I cooked comfort food when my own stomach twisted. I sat with her through the silence that weighed as much as stone.

People tried to offer words. Some were helpful. Some were not. I learned how easily platitudes crumble in the heat. I learned who could sit in the ash without looking away. I learned how much rage my body could hold without exploding. I carried a private wish to hurt him that I had to keep casting into the fire and watching it burn. I carried shame even though I knew I had done nothing wrong. Shame is sticky like smoke. It clings to your hair and your clothes, and it takes time to wash away.

There were practical things to do. I changed the locks. I made a safety plan with my children. I spoke to the school. I watched the windows a little longer than before. I checked the doors twice. I kept the oxygen tube in place and still taught myself to be a fortress. Healing is never elegant. It is a stack of small choices that do not feel like enough and yet become the path.

Therapy helped, but it was not a magic key. It was a room where we could say the words without choking. It was a place where my daughter could name the fear and the fury and the grief. It was a place where I could say I wanted to hurt him and not be jailed by that confession. Our therapist told us that our brains were doing exactly what brains do after trauma. We were scanning for threats. We were rewiring. We were learning that the world could be dangerous and still full of people who love us. We practiced grounding. We named five things in a room. We counted breaths. We held fingers. We cried. We laughed at small things because laughter felt like a tiny liberation.

The fire changed our relationship. At first, we clung to each other. Then, as she moved into late teenage years, she pulled back. Distance can be a way to feel control when your body was once taken out of your own control. I respected her space, and I stayed present. I learned to say I am here without forcing closeness. I learned the art of standing nearby with my hands open.

Over time, we found our way back to ease. Today we are friends as well as mother and daughter. We do things together. We share food. We share jokes. There are days when the ash blows up again, but we know how to wipe our faces and keep going.

The cracks in me remained. I did not trust men for a long time. I could not. The idea of dating felt like walking into a field of hidden mines. I was afraid to leave my kids anywhere. I was afraid of the sound of keys in a door that I had not turned. I was afraid of sleep because sleep felt like surrender. Even now, a piece of that fire lives in my chest. I have made peace with the fact that some flames are part of me. They are not burning me alive anymore. They are a pilot light that reminds me to keep watch.

Wolves can wear wool, smooth talk, and smiles. They can hold grocery bags. They can cut hair and charm mothers and play with children and still carry a darkness they hide behind borrowed identities. That realization changed how I moved in the world. I started to verify more. I asked different questions. I checked more doors. I still believe in good men. I know them. I am related to them. I have been loved well. But I also know that evil can be polite. It can be punctual. It can say grace before dinner. That is the part I wish I did not have to know.

There are sounds from that season I cannot forget. The metallic click of handcuffs in my hallway. The muffled sob of my daughter in the clinic. The whisper of my son sitting in a squad car, not understanding but understanding enough. The low, calm voice of the woman with the badge who refused to rush me. The phone line that carried my daughter's courage to her father. Some images still move behind my eyes. The way my daughter's hand looked small inside mine. The way the clinic's lights made everything too bright. The shape of the ottoman in the living room, where laughter used to live. The way morning looked cruelly ordinary outside the window while our lives burned inside.

183

If you ask where God was, I will tell you God was in the timing. He was in the way, my daughter did not scream because she knew my rage would make me a prisoner. He was in my sister answering the phone late at night and getting to my daughter. He was the officer who let me take my medication before he took me outside. He was in the hands of a nurse who did her job without making my child feel like a specimen. He was the judge who handed down a sentence long enough to keep other girls safe. He was in the years that followed when healing came in fractions.

Sometimes I imagine the house in Park Hill the way it was that night before everything broke. The square ottoman with a blanket tossed over it. The sound of a punchline that made my son giggle. The comfort of falling asleep in my own bed. I hold that image, and I hold the other one where a door is cracked open and a hand reaches where it does not belong. Both are true. Both belong to our story. The fire burned through both and left us standing in new ground.

I still have days where I relive the moment, I saw him in my bed and the world tilted. I still have days where I replay what would have happened if I had woken up while he was hurting her. I do not stay in those scenes. I let the fire pass through, and I look for the water. The water is my daughter's voice when she jokes with me now. It is my son's tenderness, the same tenderness he showed when he got ice for my eyes after his kidnapping. It is the way my body is strong again. It is the way my spirit bends but does not break. It is the way our family keeps choosing love.

Healing is not forgetting. Healing is remembering without being owned by the memory. I can walk past a leather couch and not feel sick. I can sit in a clinic waiting room and breathe. I can hear a knock at the door and not freeze. I can tell this story without swallowing glass. That is the work we did. That is the work we still do.

For the mothers reading this who know fire, I want to say this. You are not responsible for the crimes of another. You are not a failed guardrail because someone drove through you. You are a mountain that has already survived eruptions. You can stand again. You can raise your children in a world that has teeth and still feed them hope. You can build a new house inside your chest and invite light in. You can love without pretending that bad things do not happen. You can choose to trust selectively and still keep your heart open.

There is a point in every eruption when the lava cools and becomes land. It is not the land you started with. It is rough and new and black as night. But it is land. It can hold a home. It can grow a garden. It can be a path. We live there now. On ground that was once fire. On a foundation that started with ash. On a story that refuses to end at the worst chapter. We live and love and laugh and sometimes cry. We carry the past as a fact, not a prison. We name our scars and we bless our survival.

If I could speak to that version of me who woke up to sunlight that was not there and a voice saying Denver Police, I would tell her to breathe. I would tell her that she will make it through the next hour and then the next. I would tell her that she will hold her daughter, survive the clinic, call the chaplain, sign the statements, sit through the hearings, and find a way to sleep again. I would tell her that one day her daughter will call just to talk about nothing and everything, and she will realize that the sound of that laugh is proof that the fire did not win.

This is the truth. The volcano erupted. It burned what it touched. And still, we rose from the ashes.

When the Ground Trembles
Pause. Breathe. Reflect.

Some fires arrive without warning. They burn through walls, words, and innocence, leaving nothing untouched. Yet even volcanoes cool, and from the blackened soil, new life begins to grow. This reflection is your space to honor the flames and begin rebuilding on new ground.

Healing after devastation is not linear. It is breath by breath. Word by word. The smoke clears slowly, but it *does* clear. You survived the eruption. Now it's time to reclaim your footing.

Grounding Tools

1. The Five Senses Anchor
When memories rise like heat, find something around you for each of your senses:

- 5 things you can see
- 4 things you can touch
- 3 things you can hear
- 2 things you can smell
- 1 thing you can taste

Name each one out loud until your body remembers: *I am here. I am safe now.*

2. Lava to Land Visualization

Close your eyes. Picture molten fire cooling into solid ground. Imagine your breath as rain falling on it—steam rising, then calm. Whisper: *I am rebuilding. I am whole.*

3. The Body Reset

When you feel anger, guilt, or grief rise in your chest:

- Place your right hand on your heart.

- Inhale deeply for a count of 4.

- Hold for 4.

- Exhale for 6.
  Repeat until the tremor in your body softens.

-

🌼 Healing Tools

- **Therapy as Shelter:** Therapy is the room where your heart can exhale. Speak your truth there without judgment or correction.

- **Creative Release:** Write, paint, sing, or dance out the words you can't yet say. Creation reclaims what destruction tried to steal.

- **Community:** Healing requires witnesses. Find safe people—mentors, support groups, friends—who can hold space without needing to fix you.

- **Affirmation Practice:** Start or end your day by saying: *I am not what happened to me. I am what I choose to become.*

-

Journal Prompt 1: What does survival look like for you now, after the fire? Describe it through your senses.

Journal Prompt 2: Who stood in the flames with you, and who walked away? How do you want to honor those who stayed?

Journal Prompt 3: What would forgiveness look like—not for the person who caused harm, but for yourself?

Journal Prompt 4: Imagine your future self-standing on land that has cooled. What does she see? What has she built there?

Journal Prompt 5: Write a letter to your inner child or inner mother, offering the comfort and safety you both needed then.

Closing Thought

Fire destroys, but it also forges. It refines gold and strengthens stone. You are both, the precious and the powerful.

Let this be your new mantra: *The volcano did not end me. It revealed the fire within me that cannot be extinguished.*

Latricia Ferris

When peace finally found me, it sounded like silence after thunder

Beyond the Storm

After the Storm: Gardens of Fire

"Some flowers only grow in the soil left behind by volcanoes."

Affirmation: From fire, we created color. From pain, we built peace. From ash, we rose in love.

The years after the fire felt like sunlight breaking through clouds that had hung too long. I had spent so much time surviving that I almost forgot what it felt like to live without fear. But healing has a rhythm of its own. It doesn't rush. It creeps in softly, like morning light through blinds, until one day you realize you can breathe again. That's what life began to feel like with my daughter, Danajha. The storm had not taken her; it had transformed her.

When she was thirteen, I first discovered her voice. It was a regular afternoon, laundry tumbling in the dryer, the hum of normal life filling the house. Then came a sound so powerful, so soulful, I froze. It was a voice that felt too seasoned for a child, full of ache and glory. I thought it was the radio, some new artist I hadn't heard before. But when I stepped into the room, it wasn't a record or a song from the speakers; it was my baby girl. Standing there barefoot, eyes closed, singing her own melody into the air as if she was releasing every part of herself that had ever been silenced.

That sound carried something holy. It reminded me that even after the volcano, even after all that ash, something beautiful could still bloom. Her gift became the first sign of the garden to come.

School came easily to her. Her birthday made her the youngest in her class, but her mind and determination always made her stand out. Teachers called her mature, driven, and a natural leader. She made the honor roll year after year, and I saw the way she approached everything like it was art, focused, steady, with heart. Watching her grow into her own brilliance was like watching God paint in real time.

By sixteen, her fire had turned to ambition. She got her first job at Elitch Gardens, smiling her way through long summer days. But it wasn't long before she outgrew that, moving on to Chick-fil-A, where she rose from cashier to team leader in record time. I still remember her coming home one day, proud but humble, telling me how she had to train new employees, grown men and women twice her age, on how to lead with kindness. Even after leaving the company, the owners stayed in touch, proof that her light leaves marks wherever it shines.

When graduation came, she looked at me with that same quiet confidence she's always had and said, "Mama, I want to start my own business." There was no hesitation in her voice, no fear. Just purpose. She started with cakes, small at first, birthday orders, and family events. I'd see her late at night in the kitchen, measuring flour, perfecting frosting, focused in a way that reminded me of myself when I'm building something from scratch. The first time she handed over a finished cake, I saw that spark again, the same one I heard in her voice years before. The woman who ordered it called crying later, saying it was too beautiful to cut. That's when I knew my daughter had found her calling.

Her business grew faster than we imagined. Word spread, followers came, and before long, she became known as "The Cake Lady." Her cakes weren't just desserts; they were masterpieces. Buttercream roses that looked alive, marble fondant that could've been sculpted by an artist. But it wasn't just the cakes; it was the energy she poured into them. She made people feel celebrated. She made moments memorable.

Then she began catering full meals, taking her talents even further. Her kitchen became a place of joy and creation. The aroma of jerk chicken, garlic butter shrimp, and baked mac and cheese filled her home. Every dish came with love, a seasoning only she knew how to use. Soon after, she launched her party planning business, turning empty spaces into dreamscapes of light and laughter. She handled everything with her best friend, decor, food, music, and ambiance, which made it look effortless. I watched her build empires with her hands, proof that creativity runs deep in our lineage.

Through it all, our bond deepened. We talked more than ever. About business, love, God, and everything in between. She became not just my daughter but my mirror, strong, resilient, and grounded. Sometimes, she'd call just to say, "Mama, you've taught me so much." Other times, she'd remind me to rest, to stop overworking, to celebrate the moment. It's a strange and beautiful thing when your child begins to mother you, too.

The volcano that once tore through our world had become the very soil where her dreams took root.

When I turned forty, I wanted to mark it with something big. I told myself I wanted to go to Jamaica, to feel the ocean on my skin and the sun on my shoulders. Before I could finish the thought, Danajha said, "I'm coming too." That's who she is, never letting me walk alone into any new chapter. We booked the flights together, packed our suitcases with laughter, and decided to make it a trip we'd never forget.

Jamaica was everything I dreamed of and more. The air was heavy with salt and rhythm, the kind of place where even silence had music. We explored the island, the hills green as emeralds, the sea shimmering like liquid glass. We danced to reggae on the beach, ate jerk chicken that was smoky and sweet, and laughed until our stomachs hurt. One day, we sat on a private beach, the sun stretching across the water like gold silk. Waves crashed softly, and for a while, we just listened. Then she said, "Mama, I'm proud of us."

Her words caught me off guard. "Of us?" I asked.

"Yeah," she said, smiling at the horizon. "You could've let life break you. But you didn't. You showed me how to turn pain into power. That's why I know I can do anything."

I turned to look at her, the sunlight soft on her face, and I realized she wasn't just my daughter anymore; she was my legacy.

After Jamaica, we went to the Cayman Islands. The water there was impossibly blue, like the earth had been holding its breath for centuries. We decided to swim with dolphins and sea turtles, something I'd always wanted to do. I was nervous for her; she didn't know how to swim. But that didn't stop her. She laughed, threw on a life vest, and said, "Don't worry, I'll figure it out." And she did. Watching her doggy paddle through that turquoise water, fearless and free, I couldn't help but smile. That's my baby, I thought. The same girl who once survived the unthinkable was now floating in paradise.

Later that evening, we sat poolside, sipping fruity drinks and listening to live music. The air smelled like coconut oil and warm sea breeze. She leaned back in her chair, looked at me, and said, "Mama, this is the life we deserve." And she was right. For the first time in a long time, I felt it too, the peace of a woman who has weathered every storm and come out shining.

Those trips became more than vacations; they were symbols of survival. Proof that beauty can come from devastation. We laughed until we cried, danced barefoot on sand still warm from the day, and talked about everything we'd been through. We weren't running from the past; we were honoring it by living fully in the present.

Now, at twenty-five, Danajha is unstoppable. Her baking business thrives. She caters weddings, birthdays, and galas. Her social media is filled with clients praising her creativity, her heart, and her attention to detail. She manages her team, books events months in advance, and still finds time to have fun with her family. She's proof that success doesn't just come from talent; it comes from grit, discipline, and heart.

She has become the kind of woman every mother hopes her daughter will be: confident, compassionate, driven, and unshakably kind. She gives back to others, mentors young entrepreneurs, and moves through the world with grace. And what I love most is how she still carries that same spark. The same joy that filled our house when she sang at thirteen.

Our relationship now is built on mutual respect and love. We travel, dream, and build together. Sometimes she'll say, "Mama, imagine where we'll be in five years." And I smile because I already know, it'll be somewhere even brighter.

Every time I see her, I see proof that pain can be turned into beauty. She is my greatest testimony. The volcano erupted, but it did not destroy us. It forged something indestructible, a bond that fire could never break.

The storms are behind me now, but their lessons remain. I've learned that motherhood isn't about perfection; it's about persistence. It's about standing in the ashes and saying, "We will rise again." Watching Danajha live her truth, fearlessly and fully, has healed places in me I didn't know were still cracked. She is the garden that grew from fire, the bloom that reminds me why I never gave up.

If you're reading this, know that healing is possible. You can turn the smoke into sunlight. You can dance again. You can breathe again. You can love again. There is life after the volcano. There is beauty in the aftermath.

We are proof of that.

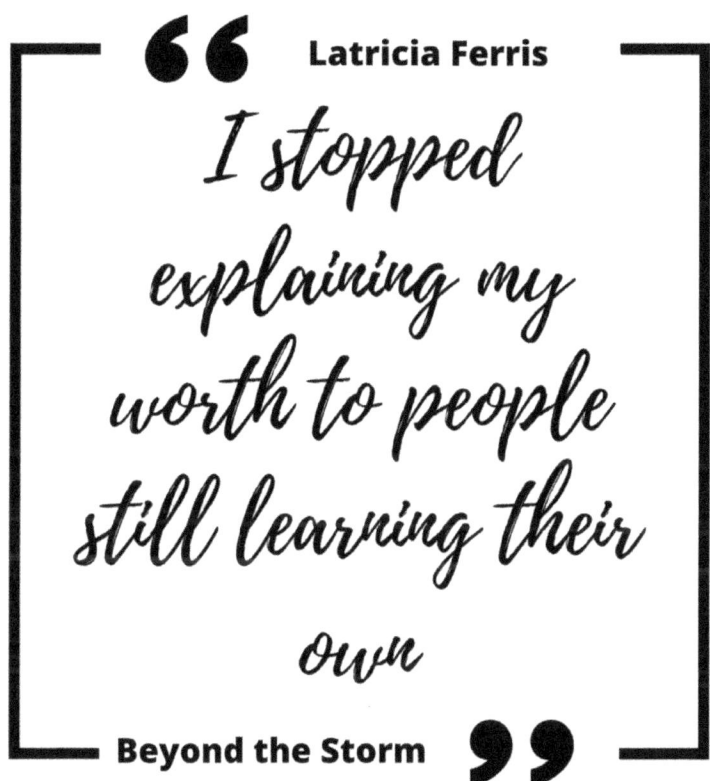

Latricia Ferris

I stopped explaining my worth to people still learning their own

Beyond the Storm

198

Beyond the Storm: Pain Turned into Power

"I am a phoenix who rose from the ashes."

Affirmation: My pain became my paintbrush, my tears became my water, and from every storm I created light.

The world is quiet after the storm. The air still hums with memory, like thunder echoing in my bones. I stand at the edge of everything I've survived, breathing in the peace that only comes when you've walked through fire and realized you were the flame all along.

This is what healing sounds like, not a trumpet, not a choir, but a whisper between you and God saying, "You made it."

There are mornings I still wake up remembering the noise, the shaking ground, the breaking hearts, the nights I prayed until my throat was dry. But now, I paint. I pray with color, I heal in strokes of acrylic and gold. My art is my altar, and every canvas holds a piece of what I've overcome.

I light candles, soft music rising like breath from the speakers, my crystals resting in my pockets like old friends. There's always a vase of yellow flowers beside me, sunlight in bloom, a promise that joy will always find its way back home.

Yellow, because it's the color of faith. Yellow, because it's how I remind myself that even after lightning splits the sky, the sun still dares to shine.

When I paint, it's not just paint, it's prayer. Each brushstroke says thank you. Each color remembers. Some pieces are goddesses with halos of light, others are self-portraits with tired eyes and wings too heavy to fold. Sometimes I paint little versions of the girl I used to be, the one who still believed the world was kind, so I can tell her, "Look, baby, we made it."

I've turned my pain into portraits, my sorrow into shapes that shimmer. Art became my medicine, the language I speak when words won't come. And Yahweh sits with me while I work. I feel Him in the rhythm of my breathing, in the way my hands don't shake anymore. I feel my ancestors, too, watching from the corners of my studio, their love stretching through time, whispering, "Keep going. This is sacred work."

I think about my children often while I paint. Not just who they are, but who they've become.

Aron, my miracle boy, whose story began in chaos but bloomed in brilliance. The same child who once trembled in fear became a man who creates beauty through music. He turned frequencies into freedom, pain into sound that travels the world. When I hear his songs, I hear resilience wrapped in rhythm, the echo of survival played on repeat. He built a production company before most even knew their path, a living example that trauma doesn't have to end in tragedy; it can be transformed into art that heals others.

And then there's J'Honesty, my baby by love, not by blood. He came into my life like a gentle sunrise, reminding me that motherhood has no limits. He filled spaces I didn't know were empty. When I look at him, I see that family is not just who we are born to, it's who we choose to nurture, who chooses to stay. He's my reminder that love can rewrite the story.

And my daughter, my reflection, Danajha. There are moments I watch her move through life, and I swear I'm looking at light in human form. At thirteen, I discovered her voice, not metaphorically, but literally. That day, I thought a new artist had come on the radio. The voice was powerful like Adele, soulful like Patti LaBelle. I walked into the room and froze. It wasn't the radio. It was her. My baby. Singing with her eyes closed, as if heaven had slipped through her throat.

Sometimes I think the storms were just lessons in disguise. Each one stripped me bare until all that was left was truth. And from that truth, I built Dream, Believe & Imagine. Not as a brand, but as a calling. It's the home for every lesson, every scar, every victory. It's the proof that the sun really does rise again. My storms taught me leadership. My pain taught me empathy. My healing taught me purpose. Now, I pour that wisdom into others, helping them rebuild their own lives from ashes.

When I stand on a stage or mentor people, I don't just speak, I testify. I tell them that power doesn't come from what you've avoided, it comes from what you've survived. And baby, I've survived it all.

I used to ask, "Why me?" Now I ask, "What for?" And the answer is always the same: to teach, to heal, to shine.

There's a moment that comes after every storm, when the clouds break and sunlight touches the ruins. The ground still smokes, the air still carries the scent of fire, but new life starts pushing through the cracks. That's where I live now, in the in-between. The space where the storm has passed, but the soil still remembers.

I've learned that rebirth isn't a single moment; it's a daily choice. To get up. To create. To love again. To forgive yourself for not knowing better back then. To trust that beauty can still come from broken things.

When I look around my home, I see my paintings on the walls, faces of goddesses and warriors, women with fire in their eyes, and halos of gold. They're not just art; they're mirrors. Every stroke says, you did it. You're still here.

And I buy myself yellow flowers every week, a promise to never forget the light. I place them beside my canvases and whisper a prayer of gratitude, because I know now that the storms weren't meant to destroy me. They were meant to reveal me.

If you're reading this, and you're still standing in your storm, listen to me. You are not broken beyond repair. You are the proof that new life grows from shattered ground. The pain you feel today is not your forever; it's your becoming. One day you'll look back and see that this, too, was sacred.

You will rise. Not the same, but stronger, softer, wiser. You will find beauty in places you once feared. You will forgive yourself. And when you do, you'll shine so bright that others will find their way by your light.

This, this is what it means to go beyond the storm. Not to forget it, but to let it teach you how to fly.

I am the calm after chaos, the bloom after rain, the phoenix who painted her wings yellow and dared to soar again. I am a mother, artist, warrior, light. I am the echo of prayers that refused to die. And if you've ever felt lost in the thunder, remember this: you are not alone. The sun is waiting. And baby... so are your wings.

To the one reading this who has walked through storms I named, sexual assault, abuse, addiction, racism, betrayal, grief, poverty, heartbreak, this part is for you. The details of our pain may differ, but the strength it takes to rise is the same. You are not your past. You are not the worst thing that has ever happened to you. You are not the lie someone told you about your worth. You are the stormbreaker, the proof that divinity can live in a body that has known pain.

Maybe you were raised by chaos. Maybe you fought to love a parent who was lost to addiction. Maybe you've been cheated on, abandoned, or made to feel invisible. Maybe you buried someone you thought you couldn't live without. Whatever your storm looks like, I want you to know: survival itself is sacred. Every breath you take after pain is a rebellion against darkness.

You are still here. That means purpose is still breathing through you.

Your story does not end in the wreckage. You get to choose what rises from it. You get to decide whether you stay buried or bloom. You have the right to rest. You have the right to rebuild. You have the right to joy again.

When I say pain turned to power, I don't mean pretending it didn't hurt. I mean, learning that even broken wings can still carry you higher. Healing is not perfection. It's permission to start again. Every time you forgive, every time you show love when the world tries to make you hard, every time you refuse to quit, that is power. That is victory.

You are worthy. Worthy of love that doesn't hurt. Worthy of peace that lasts. Worthy of life beyond survival. You are not damaged, you are divine in progress.

The world tried to name you by your wounds, but God already named you by your purpose. And your purpose is bigger than your pain. Maybe you don't see it yet, but it's there, waiting under the rubble like a seed waiting for light.

I built Dream, Believe & Imagine because I wanted to give others a map out of the storm. But you already carry your compass within. The same spirit that got me through will get you through. You just have to remember who you are: chosen, powerful, and loved.

One day, you'll tell your story without trembling. You'll use your voice to guide someone else through their darkness. You'll see that the cracks in your soul are where the light got in. And when you do, promise me you'll lift someone else. Because that's what healing is, it's not just surviving, it's reaching back for the next soul still caught in the rain.

We are all artists here. Pain gave us the palette, and love gives us the brush. What you create with it is up to you.

If you've ever been silenced, speak. If you've ever been hurt, heal loudly. If you've ever felt unseen, shine anyway. If they counted you out, rise higher. If they tried to bury you, bloom. You are not behind; you are being refined. You are the phoenix, the sun after the storm, the living proof that grace is real.

And when the storms come again, and they will, remember that you have already learned how to dance in the rain.

So, light your candles. Play your music. Paint your prayers. Plant your seeds. Tell your story. And never, ever forget: you are not the storm. You are the sky after.

Latricia Ferris

The storm coundl't kill me because I was born from one

Beyond the Storm

207

Latricia Ferris is a visionary, mentor, and artist whose life's mission is to help others transform pain into power. She is the founder and CEO of **Dream, Believe & Imagine**, a C-Corporation dedicated to empowering individuals to heal, grow, and reimagine life through mentorship, workshops, and motivational speaking.

Latricia's story is one of resilience, faith, and purpose. A proud mother of two biological children, **Danajha and Aron**, and her bonus son **J'Honesty**, she has built her legacy on the belief that storms are not meant to destroy us but to awaken the strength within. Through every chapter of her life, from surviving trauma and heartbreak to rising as a respected community leader, Latricia has turned her scars into stories that inspire and heal.

Her passion for service and leadership extends far beyond her writing. With over twenty years of experience mentoring youth and professionals, she leads and serves on several community boards, including **Bridge the Gap Colorado** and formerly **Disability: IN**. She is also a **WICT mentor**, dedicated to helping women grow in confidence and leadership.

Latricia's commitment to empowerment and education has earned her numerous recognitions, including being named **Top Black Educator in Colorado** by *My Black Colorado* and receiving the **Green Apple Award** from *Junior Achievement* for mentoring over 500 students. In 2025, she was honored with the **TrailblazHER Award** from the *LeadHERship Gala* for pioneering change and inspiring future generations.

As a volunteer and mentor at **Florence Crittenton**, Latricia works closely with young mothers, guiding them to see their worth and build the futures they deserve. Her work in community advocacy, mentorship, and empowerment continues to ripple across generations.

When Latricia isn't mentoring or leading, she creates. As a self-taught artist, she draws, paints, and designs digital art that reflects her emotions and faith. Her pieces, from portraits of goddesses to magical creatures and childhood cartoons, serve as living reminders of resilience, faith, and beauty born from pain. Her art, much like her words, tells a story of survival, rebirth, and divine transformation.

In addition to *Beyond the Storm*, Latricia is the author of an upcoming children's book that continues her mission of spreading light, self-belief, and imagination.

Through her art, her voice, and her leadership, Latricia Ferris continues to remind others that no matter how fierce the storm, healing is always possible. Her life is proof that pain can be the seed of purpose and that beauty can always rise from broken ground.

To connect, collaborate, or learn more about her programs and speaking engagements, visit **www.dreambelieveimagine.com** or follow **@DreamBelieveImagine** across social media platforms.

www.ingramcontent.com/pod-product-compliance
Lightning Source LLC
Chambersburg PA
CBHW050446150626
46551CB00029B/1800